An Adirondack Sampler

An Adirondack Sampler

Day Hikes For All Seasons

BRUCE WADSWORTH

Adirondack Mountain Club
Lake George, New York

Published by the Adirondack Mountain Club, Inc.
814 Goggins Road, Lake George, NY 12845-4117
Visit our web site: **www.adk.org**

Copyright © 1979, 1988, 1991, 1996 by the Adirondack Mountain Club, Inc.

Cover and text design: Christopher Kuntze
Cover art: Rachel O'Meara
Photographs by the author unless noted otherwise.

First edition 1979
    reprinted with revisions 1983
    reprinted 1984
    reprinted with revisions 1986
Second edition 1988
    reprinted with revisions 1990
Third edition 1992
    reprinted with revisions 1994
Fourth edition 1996
    reprinted with revisions 1998, 2001
    reprinted 2004
    reprinted with revisions 2007
    reprinted with revisions 2008

Library of Congress Cataloging-in-Publication Data
Wadsworth, Bruce.
    An Adirondack sampler : day hikes for all seasons / by Bruce C.
Wadsworth. — 4th ed.
        p. cm.
    Includes index.
    ISBN 10: 0-935272-83-6
    ISBN 13: 978-0-935272-83-3
    1. Hiking—New York (State)—Adirondack Mountains—Guidebooks.
    2. Adirondack Mountains (N.Y.)—Guidebooks. I. Title.
GV199.42.N652A348   1996
796.5'1'097475—dc20   96-20517
                                    CIP

Printed in the United States of America
15   13

Dedication

This guidebook is dedicated to the fire tower observers of the Adirondack Park. Many trails used by the hiker today exist only because they lead, or once led, to a tower staffed by these memorable men and women. The strong, positive feelings of many New Yorkers for their Adirondacks must, like mine, be partly due to happy memories of times spent with fire observers on mountain tops.

Fire observers have guarded our forests since 1912, when the first fire towers were authorized. Today, air surveillance and other means of fire detection have reduced, and are continuing to reduce, their numbers. One of the saddest parts about writing this book was finding so many closed towers and foundations of removed towers on mountain peaks.

On the other hand, it is heartening to note that since the first edition of this guide in 1979, a resurgence of interest has occurred in the use of fire towers as historic and educational resources. Several of the towers that grace the summits described in this book, have been restored and reopened to the public.

Time stands still for no one, but let us not forget the dedication and lonely service of the fire observers. These philosophers and raconteurs of the peaks do much to add color and character to the mountain experiences of those of us who are privileged to visit their towers.

Acknowledgments

It's hard to believe this guide has been introducing hiking trails of the Adirondacks to recreationists since 1979. At the time of its inception, there was a concentration of hiking in the High Peaks that was detrimental both to the ecology of the area and to hikers' maximum enjoyment of the outdoors. Trails were becoming heavily eroded, parking was getting to be a problem and a sense of solitude was difficult to find on major trails.

Although everyone seemed to know about Mount Marcy and the eastern half of the High Peaks Wilderness, very few hikers were aware that there are over 2 million more acres of Forest Preserve that also have trails, lakes and mountains to explore. Two important purposes of this book were—and still are—to inform day hikers of some of the best hiking trails outside of the High Peaks and to encourage them to use them. Much more suitable for beginning hikers, these "little" mountains and less rugged trails provide opportunities for wonderful outings. Happily, the book has continued to serve these purposes while also providing basic information for enjoyment of outing experiences.

Many changes in hiking trails, safety concerns and equipment have occurred since the printing of the first *Sampler*. Updates, new trails or other revisions are introduced to each new edition or printing as needed. I thank both guide users and several long-time hiking friends who have noted trail changes and were kind enough to inform me. A special note of thanks must be given to the forest rangers into whose hands have been entrusted the care of the trails and regions described in this book. Their help has been irreplaceable.

Andrea Masters continues to provide expert professional expertise as director of publications of the Adirondack Mountain Club. Her growing staff is much appreciated.

As always, thanks must be given to my wife, Betty, who most generally is with me on the trails, offering good ideas and much help.

We welcome your letters!

ADK and its authors make every effort to keep our guidebooks up to date, however, trail conditions are always changing. If you note an error or discrepancy, or if you wish to forward a suggestion, we welcome your input. Please write the Adirondack Mountain Club, Attn: Publications, citing book title, year of your edition (see copyright page), trail number, page number, and date of your observation. Our address is 814 Goggins Road, Lake George, NY 12845-4117. Thanks for your help.

Contents

INTRODUCTION   11
  Winter Hiking   11

HOW TO USE THIS BOOK   13
  Trip Headings   13
  Glossary   16

TRAIL HABITS AND PRACTICES   17
What Do You Need?   17
Checklist of Hiking Equipment   21
  Trail Manners   21
  Campfires   21
  Fire Towers   22
  Safety   22

THE ADIRONDACKS   23

THE ADIRONDACK MOUNTAIN CLUB   27

Lake George and Southeast Section   29
The Tongue Mountain Range (1–3)   29
  1. Five Mile Mountain   30
  2. Fifth Peak   32
  3. Northwest Bay to Montcalm Point   33
  4. Buck Mountain   34
  5. Black Mountain Loop   36
  6. Hadley Mountain   38
  7. Crane Mountain   39
  8. Pharaoh Mountain   41

Indian Lake and South Section   43
  9. Snowy Mountain   43
  10. Echo Cliffs at Panther Mountain   44
  11. Chimney Mountain   46
  12. Wilcox Lake Walk   47
  13. Cod Pond   49
  14. Sawyer Mountain   50

Eagle Bay and Blue Mountain Section   53
  15. Rondaxe (Bald) Mountain   53
  16. Moss Lake Circuit Trail   54
  17. Windfall Pond Walk and Loop Option   56
  18. Black Bear Mountain   57

19.	Blue Mountain	60
20.	Cascade Pond	62

Minerva–Newcomb Section — 65
21.	Rankin Pond	65
22.	Boreas River Walk	66
23.	Vanderwhacker Mountain	66
	Roosevelt Memorial Tablet	69
24.	Newcomb Visitor Interpretive Center	70
25.	Goodnow Mountain	70

Keene–Keene Valley Section — 73
26.	Sunrise Trail to Gilligan Mountain	73
27.	The Brothers Trail and Loop Option	74
28.	Hopkins Mountain via Mossy Cascade Brook	77
29.	Hurricane Mountain	78
30.	Balanced Rocks on Pitchoff Mountain	79
	Stagecoach Rock	80
31.	Noonmark Mountain from Round Pond	82
32.	The Crow Mountains	83

Lake Placid, Saranac Lake, and Paul Smiths Section — 85
33.	Ampersand Mountain	85
34.	Baker Mountain	86
35.	Scarface Mountain	87
36.	Haystack Mountain	89
37.	Owen and Copperas Ponds Walk	91
38.	Wanika Falls	92
39.	Mt. Jo	93
40.	Paul Smiths Visitor Interpretive Center	96
41.	St. Regis Mountain	96

Cranberry Lake, Wanakena, and West Section — 99
	Sunday Rock	99
42.	Cat Mountain	100
43.	Brandy Brook Flow	102
44.	Bear Mountain	104
45.	Arab Mountain	107

North–Northeast Section — 109
46.	Poke-O-Moonshine Mountain	109
47.	Lyon Mountain	110
48.	Silver Lake Mountain	111
49.	Azure (Blue) Mountain	113
50.	Debar Mountain	114

Index	117
Index of People	119

Hike Locator Map

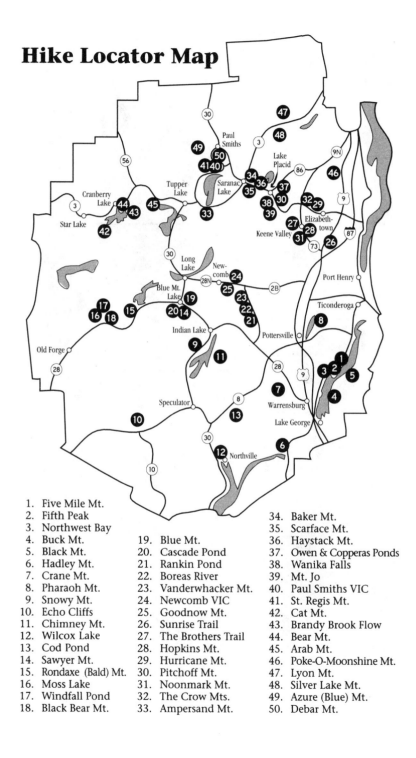

1. Five Mile Mt.
2. Fifth Peak
3. Northwest Bay
4. Buck Mt.
5. Black Mt.
6. Hadley Mt.
7. Crane Mt.
8. Pharaoh Mt.
9. Snowy Mt.
10. Echo Cliffs
11. Chimney Mt.
12. Wilcox Lake
13. Cod Pond
14. Sawyer Mt.
15. Rondaxe (Bald) Mt.
16. Moss Lake
17. Windfall Pond
18. Black Bear Mt.

19. Blue Mt.
20. Cascade Pond
21. Rankin Pond
22. Boreas River
23. Vanderwhacker Mt.
24. Newcomb VIC
25. Goodnow Mt.
26. Sunrise Trail
27. The Brothers Trail
28. Hopkins Mt.
29. Hurricane Mt.
30. Pitchoff Mt.
31. Noonmark Mt.
32. The Crow Mts.
33. Ampersand Mt.

34. Baker Mt.
35. Scarface Mt.
36. Haystack Mt.
37. Owen & Copperas Ponds
38. Wanika Falls
39. Mt. Jo
40. Paul Smiths VIC
41. St. Regis Mt.
42. Cat Mt.
43. Brandy Brook Flow
44. Bear Mt.
45. Arab Mt.
46. Poke-O-Moonshine Mt.
47. Lyon Mt.
48. Silver Lake Mt.
49. Azure (Blue) Mt.
50. Debar Mt.

Introduction

"It's a great thing these days to leave civilization for awhile."

ROBERT MARSHALL, 1937

An Adirondack Sampler was written as an introduction to that vast and marvelous region called the Adirondacks. It invites you to visit the trails, streams, and mountains of the largest park in the contiguous United States and will guide you into some of the nicest places in the Adirondacks reachable on foot.

The *Sampler* was planned for the single-day forest traveler; most of the hikes can be completed in six hours or less. It is for those who are just beginning the adventure of hiking as well as for those who have traveled the more rugged high peaks and are now seeking less challenging, but just as enjoyable, journeys. It is ideal for family outings. The winter hiker, especially the snowshoer, will find the *Sampler* a welcome companion.

This guidebook contains hikes in all regions of the Adirondack Park. It is not necessary, or even desirable, to begin one's climbing experience in the high peaks around Mt. Marcy. Too often the neophyte in the High Peaks lacks either the stamina or the skills—or both—needed to enjoy such trips. The hikes described here will enable the beginner to gain the know-how necessary for longer excursions while fully enjoying the forest experience.

The *Sampler* is for the many day hikers who simply want to enjoy the out-of-doors on a fine weekend. For you, the Adirondacks can be summed up by the deer that magically appears at lakeside at day's end, by a cascading brook in springtime, by the falling leaves of autumn hardwoods. For you, a quiet place with a beautiful view encourages contemplation; a rippling stream evokes pleasant thoughts. Not for you a crowded trail to Mt. Marcy.

The Adirondacks are full of rippling streams, quiet ponds, and hundreds of seldom-trod trails. Dozens of mountains patiently await the occasional visitor. Go and visit them. One of them is sure to become your own special place.

Winter Hiking

Winter hiking, snowshoeing, and cross-country skiing are all becoming very popular. Many of the trips included in this guidebook are excellent for these activities.

One must keep in mind that hiking in winter is far different from summer hiking. Travel times will be much longer. Energy demands are greater. Clothing requirements are more strict. Tolerances for error are much less. Winter in the woods is beautiful, but do not take preparation for even an afternoon's outing lightly. Weather conditions in the Adirondacks can be as severe as those found anywhere else on this earth. Wet rains and freezing winds can be disastrous. Whiteouts can turn a short mountain climb into an overnight struggle for survival.

The novice should gain winter experience in organized groups such as the chapters of the Adirondack Mountain Club and with knowledgeable individuals. Do not go out alone in the winter. It is recommended, in summer or winter, to have at least four members in your group as a minimum for safety. In case of injury this permits one person to remain with the injured party while the other two go for help.

How To Use This Book

Trip Headings

DIFFICULTY. Each hike description in this guidebook begins with a basic listing of information that will enable you to approximate its difficulty. Distances and elevations do not require evaluation except to determine if the trips are within your capability. The data are quite accurate. Your judgment must be used to make best use of some of the other information.

Times for round trips are generally conservative. Some people walk faster than others, and even the same person may push on rapidly when a storm beckons overhead but will tarry while looking at wildflowers on a warm spring day. Are you in good physical condition? Do you have a small child along with you who may have to be carried from time to time? These are variables that must be considered. After a trip or two you should be able to compare travel times on past outings and make adjustments from the given travel times to determine the travel times that best fit your style of hiking.

What is "steep" to one person is "easy" to another. No two people seem to evaluate trail difficulty in the same manner. In the trail descriptions an attempt has been made to standardize the use of terms relating to steepness. Five terms are used: gradual, moderate, moderately steep, steep, and very steep. The terms are based upon relative grade, not on ease of travel. How "easy" the grades will seem to you depends upon your physical condition, experience, and mental outlook.

DISTANCE AND ELEVATION. New topographic maps are printed with metric units, while most older maps currently in use have the English units. Therefore, distances and elevations have been expressed both in English and metric units. Metric units are placed in parentheses following the English units. The abbreviation *m* means meters in the metric system; *km* means kilometers. One kilometer equals one thousand meters. Indicated distances have been kept to a minimum in this book. Most trips are fairly short and the intermediate distances are not really essential for following the route.

MAPS. Some page maps are included in this book. United States Geological Survey (USGS) topographic maps can also be used to help you locate and follow several of the trails described in this book. They often include other trails not described in this book but that may be of interest to you.

In mapping, the term *minute* is used to represent an angle measurement. There are 60 minutes in 1 degree. There are 360 degrees in any circle encompassing the earth. A 7.5-minute shows a ground area that represents 7.5 minutes of longitude x 7.5 minutes of latitude. In the

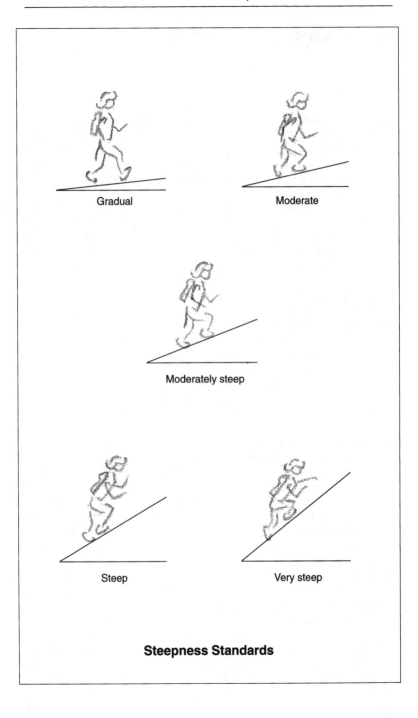

Gradual

Moderate

Moderately steep

Steep

Very steep

Steepness Standards

Adirondacks, a 7.5-minute map represents a ground distance of about 6.3 mi. (10 km) in an east–west direction and about 8.8 mi. (14 km) in a north–south direction. Occasionally, 15-minute maps are available. Such maps represent four times the ground area of a 7.5-minute map, which is often advantageous, but they are printed on a much smaller scale and thus permit far less detail.

Since 1978, a third type of map has been marketed. This is a 7.5-minute x 15-minute quadrangle using metric units. In preparation for the 1980 Olympic Games at Lake Placid, the USGS made the first maps in the United States for the Adirondack region. In effect, it is like putting two 7.5-minute maps side by side. It is expected that these maps will be the predominantly used maps of the future.

For each hike described in this book, all relevant map quadrangles are listed. Below is a legend showing symbols commonly used on the maps found in this book.

LEGEND

- - - -	Foot trail	P	Parking
== ==	Woods road	↘	Barrier
•• ••	Bushwhack	(10)	County or local route
▲	Mountain	(3)	State highway
🛖	Lean-to	(87)	Interstate highway

Glossary

Bushwhack
To make one's way through bushes or undergrowth.

Cairn
A pile of rocks or stones to mark a summit or route.

Col
The low point between two adjacent peaks.

Corduroy
A road, trail, or bridge formed by logs laid side by side transversely to facilitate crossing swampy places.

Duff
Partly decayed plant matter on a forest floor.

Hardscrabble
A very rough dirt road made up largely of rocks and small stones.

Lean-to
An open camp with overhanging roof on the open side.

Massif
A large rocky prominence.

Paint Blazes
Trail indicators painted on trees or rocks.

Tote Road
An inferior road used for hauling, such as a lumber road, often with corduroys.

Vlei
A marsh or swampy meadow (pronounced *vly*).

Trail Habits and Practices

What Do You Need?

The otherwise interested hiker is often bewildered by the wide assortment of equipment available on the market today. To be discouraged for this reason would be a great mistake. First, day hikes are not lengthy expeditions. Second, while equipment should be sturdy and dependable, it doesn't have to be expensive. Third, though there are factors that must be addressed before plunging into the forest, they are relatively few in number: comfort, adaptability to changing conditions, health, safety, and personal interests. Most people will find they already have several of the items needed for hiking. Purchase equipment that will satisfy your needs.

COMFORT. Since your feet are going to get you there, treat them kindly. Generally, the steeper the trail or the heavier the climber, the more rugged should be the footwear. Acceptable footwear should fit well, be sturdy, provide ankle support, and have good traction. Shoes or boots should be well broken in. For most of the hikes in this book, sneakers or work shoes will be quite adequate. Light or medium-weight hiking boots would be nicer to have, though. Sneakers may be fine on a flat, dry trail of a short distance, but they can become mighty uncomfortable on a muddy mountain trail that suddenly fills up with water during an unexpected deluge. Many hikers wear an outer pair of heavy woolen socks and a lighter pair of socks under them to reduce friction. Rest occasionally so your feet can cool off. Otherwise, they may present you with a blister to remind you to be more concerned with their welfare.

In everyday life most of us don't think much about walking. We get up from the table and walk to the living room, car, or kitchen. The act is over after a dozen or so steps. Hiking is considerably different. Besides having proper footwear, it helps a great deal to have your hands free. You don't mind carrying the picnic basket from the table to the car, but don't try to carry one five miles up a mountain. Put your food, sweater, and other gear in a pack of some sort. For a short trip this may be a travel bag over the shoulder. Eventually, however, you'll want a day pack. The cost, quality, and type depends upon your needs and your body build. Size can only be determined after you know what must be carried. Late fall and winter hiking require extra space for supplemental clothing. Many packs are compressible so that size can be altered. Generally, soft packs rather than external frame packs are more comfortable for day hikes. Some light internal frame packs are also excellent. Fifteen or twenty pounds are as much as a person can easily tote all day. Carry less if possible. Make sure the pack stitching is good and that stress points are double-stitched. Try on several styles to find which type feels comfortable on your back. An "occasional" hiker doesn't need the same quality gear as the "every weekend" hiker whose gear will get more wear and tear. Cost generally varies with quality.

ADAPTABILITY TO CHANGING CONDITIONS. Anyone who has spent much time in the Adirondacks has heard the old adage, "If you don't like the present weather, wait around another ten minutes and it'll change." Even when the weather doesn't change, the hiker will find it cooler in the forest than out in the meadow sun. The temperature drops and winds increase as elevation is gained. On the driest of days you'll still get soaked if you slip while crossing a stream. It is only good sense to prepare for the likely, but it is prudent to prepare for the unlikely as well.

One of the most simple, yet practical, items for adaptability is the hat. It protects you from the sun, rain, and insects. In cooler weather a wool cap will keep you warm even when wet. Wet, it will help cool you on a hot day. In the rain, its brim is a blessing. (Put some insect repellent around the brim and watch those pesky flies disappear.) Upwards to a third of your body heat can be controlled through your head. Getting warm after climbing awhile? Take your hat off. Getting cold? Put one on.

Make your equipment serve many functions. You may use a poncho to help keep you warm or protect you from the wind as well as to stay dry in the rain. Those extra socks you were wise enough to carry make pretty good mittens on a chilly day. A hood is desirable on that poncho or jacket. *The key to heat control is layering. Avoid perspiration.* Start with that golf jacket or light wool shirt you have in the closet. Consider the number of combinations a vest and rain jacket can offer. Carry items that can be taken off or added easily and make the adjustment as soon as your body indicates a change is needed. That heavy parka may be great for sitting in a cold stadium, but don't try to climb a mountain in one.

One more word is needed. The word is *hypothermia.* Briefly, hypothermia is a condition where heat loss exceeds the capability of the body to replace it. Body temperature decreases and death can result.

For this to happen, the air temperature need not be frigid. A high wind can quickly strip body heat away. Avoid cottons, which wick water and cause body heat loss. Use synthetics in the summer and wool in the winter. Avoid soaking your clothing with body perspiration. Remember the concept of clothing layering.

Should you or a companion find that gloves or other clothing items are being lost on the trail, stumbling is occurring while walking, shivering can't be controlled, thinking is difficult, or unusual responses occur when speaking, act without delay. Get hot food and drink into the person. High-energy, quickly digested food should be offered. Get the person warmed in any manner possible.

Every hiker should be familiar with the symptoms of hypothermia and what remedial action to take to prevent it. Contact the Adirondack Mountain Club for more information.

HEALTH. The forest is not the same as home. Whenever a person's environment is changed, health considerations should be examined.

Get a good night's rest before setting out on your trip. Follow that up with a good, high-energy breakfast so you'll maintain your stamina after a few hours of walking. Many hikers find it better to nibble food all through the day rather than have a single large midday meal. Hard candies, nuts, raisins and other dried fruits, sunflower seeds, granola, coconut, dried cereal, chocolate, and other readily available supermarket items make good trail food (gorp). Semi-sweet chocolate won't melt in hot weather. A fresh orange is great to have along. Avoid foods that require cooking, or you'll be bogged down with pots, pans, and a sore back.

You'll drink more water than normal when you hike. Take a filled canteen or plastic jug with you. (Unfortunately, no water source on or off the trail can be considered safe to drink due to the prevalence of the parasite *Giardia lamblia*. Carry water purification tablets in case of emergency.) Carry extra food, and carry those wrappers and containers out with you.

It is often said that God's only mistake was creating the black fly. Spring hiking calls for a suitable insect repellent. The best ones all have the active ingredient N, N-diethyl-meta-toluamide (DEET). Do not use repellent with this chemical on young children, however. By mid-July you may be tempted to leave repellents at home, but don't do it.

Carry a first-aid kit. It should contain an assortment of Band Aids, salves, small bandages, and a small pair of scissors. An Ace bandage is nice to have if an ankle is turned. In extremely warm weather salt tablets may be needed.

Should you feel a tender spot developing on your foot, care for it immediately before it becomes a blister. Moleskin patches are handy for this. Cut a small hole in the center of the patch a little larger than the sore spot. Place the patch on the skin with the hole over the tender spot. The raised patch then keeps the boot from irritating it more.

Don't forget toilet tissue. While many hiking areas have privies at campsites along the trails, don't count on one being present when you need one. Leave the trail, select an area having soft earth, and make a small hole 6–8 inches deep. Cover it with leaf litter before leaving it. Nature will take care of the rest. Be sure to avoid areas which are near waterways.

SAFETY. Emergencies do occur, but their intensity may be greatly minimized if you are prepared for them. A few basic items can make the difference between inconvenience and disaster. Do not expect someone to appear simply because help is needed. Even if you were sensible enough to tell a neighbor or friend of your intended route of travel and your expected return time, help should not be expected for several hours.

Although it may appear difficult to become lost on the trails found in this guidebook, carry it with you anyway. It has information that will help you gain insight about your trip. In some cases maps have been included with the trail descriptions. As you take your rest breaks, open your guidebook and read from it. If you have a topographical map, orient yourself and identify points of interest that are in view. Hiking is much more than simply getting from here to there. Awaken your senses to your environment. Learn more of your heritage. Become an integral part of your surroundings.

The trails in this guide are, for the most part, well marked, but you should always take a compass along. Check your compass direction before you begin your trip so you'll know which way to head should you become temporarily "misplaced." Take the time to become familiar with your compass *before* you need it.

Be sure to take plenty of dry matches. A candle greatly facilitates starting a fire in wet weather. If a fire is needed, build it on a rock base to prevent starting a ground fire in organic duff.

Every person in your group should carry a whistle. A lost child can panic. Teach him or her to sit down and use that whistle if separated from the party. The whistle can also be used to scare away a menacing animal. It's much safer than throwing things at it, which might cause it to attack you.

Time passes quickly when you're enjoying yourself. To avoid a return trip in the dark, do two things. Carry a watch, and carry a flashlight. Keep track of the time it takes you to cover different sections of your route and allow ample time to be off the trail before dark. Rely on the flashlight only for emergency use.

A small knife will have a multitude of uses. Don't wear one of those huge belt knives unless you're planning to skin a buffalo. A small knife with a fixed or locking blade will fill the bill.

Many hikers carry a space blanket. They are light, small, and can be very useful if you get caught out overnight. They can be extremely important if a person is seriously injured and must be kept warm.

Don't start filling your pockets with all these little items. Walking will be most unpleasant. Instead, make a ditty bag out of some scrap material and attach a drawstring to close it. Throw all the loose items into the little sack and dump it into the bottom of your pack. You'll know where everything is and packing becomes a cinch.

PERSONAL INTERESTS. Plan to enjoy yourself. What do you like to do? Take a camera if you like photography. Perhaps a field identification guide of flowers, birds, or animal tracks will make your trip more fun. A small pair of binoculars can make a view outstanding. Maybe you would just like to read a novel and while away the time. Whatever it is, tuck it into your pack and have a good time.

Checklist of Hiking Equipment

Map	Watch
Guidebook	Jacket with hood
Canteen	Poncho or other rain gear
Flashlight	Extra socks
Matches	Whistle
First-aid kit	Space blanket
Water purification tablets	Personal interest items
Compass	Day pack
Knife	Food and water
Insect repellent	Candle
Wool sweater/shirt	Hat
Toilet tissue	Ditty bag

Trail Manners

Remember that you are a visitor in a place of natural beauty. What you have come to see, others will come after you to see. The saying, "Take only pictures, leave only footprints," is an excellent motto to follow. Many hikers habitually carry litter bags and clear trails as they return after a trip. There are signs that the modern hiker is becoming more conscious of his personal obligation to maintain his natural surroundings. Set a good example.

Many trails are partially or totally on private lands. The continued use of these lands by the hiking public is often directly related to how the public uses that land. The trails and places of beauty must be kept litter-free and in good condition. Do your part. If you carry it in, carry it out. When possible, also be willing to carry out litter left by others.

Campfires

There is a growing ethic that open fires should not be built in the wild except in those areas specifically established for that purpose. Lean-tos normally have fire rings, as do certain camping areas. Remember that the Forest Preserve land is to be "forever wild." This means that no standing trees may be legally cut. Use dead and down wood only. While everyone enjoys a campfire at night, you'll find that camp cooking will be cleaner, faster, and can be done safely in more places if a small portable camper's stove is carried with you on overnight trips.

Fire Towers

Many trails described in this guidebook originally were built to lead to summit fire towers. Today, you may find the tower either unstaffed or removed. A word of caution about the former: Closed fire towers generally are not well maintained and may be in disrepair. They should be considered dangerous. If you should decide to climb one for a better view, use extreme care.

Safety

The hiker is reminded that trail conditions vary through time. Rains make some areas very slippery. Spring meltwaters can wash out bridges.

While trails are generally in good repair, manpower for trail maintenance is a continuing problem. It benefits the hiker to use common sense and reasonable precautions if unusual conditions are encountered.

The Adirondacks

Some particular place generally comes to mind when a person thinks about "the Adirondacks." It may be a summer camp, a favorite hiking trail, or the special view from a certain mountain top. Whatever or wherever it may be, it is almost always a relatively small geographical area with which the individual has developed intimacy. Each person creates for himself a private concept of what constitutes the "Adirondacks."

Let's take a look at the whole of the Adirondack Park for a moment. It is as large as the state of Vermont and as varied as the people who live within it. It is an Adirondacks that few people seem to know a great deal about, even though they may have gone to "their" Adirondacks for many years.

We can broadly divide the Adirondacks into two sections. The Mountain Belt consists of five parallel ranges running southwestward from Lake Champlain. They are the Luzerne Range, Kayaderosseras Range, Schroon Range, Boquet Range, and the Adirondack Range. The second great division is the Lake Region to the west of the Mountain Belt. This comparatively flat country is covered with long chains of lakes separated by rolling forests.

The Adirondacks are part of the vast Canadian Shield and are very old. Over a billion years ago, intrusions far beneath the surface of the earth melted and forced their way from Canada into the heart of this region. Then, swelling upward like a gigantic blister, the doming process which culminated in today's high peaks slowly began.

Anorthosite rock formed under these conditions. This grey-blue plagioclase feldspar with book lenses of mica is readily found throughout this area. Away from the center, more moderate forces changed the existing rock less. Around this core, gneisses are found. The alternation of different colored bands of minerals often makes them obvious to those who are looking for them. Since these geological activities changed the original rock, the rocks are said to be metamorphic.

Most metamorphic rock is more dense than the original rock from which it formed. It has experienced so much pressure that water can no longer penetrate it. Thus the winter meltwaters must drain off the surface rather than become subsurface groundwater.

Long Lake, Indian Lake, and Lake George are just a few examples of places where extensive breaks in the rock, called faults, have filled with water. The sharply angular turns that characterize so many Adirondack streams show where other rock breaks, called joint patterns, are followed by runoff waters. It seems as though every depression forms a pond.

During its most recent geological history, the Ice Age sculptured this land. Rounding off mountain tops and filling in valleys, glaciers created still more lakes. Isolated blocks of ice sank into the ground and then melted.

Kettlehole lakes, such as Heart Lake, resulted from this process. Where no drainage was possible from a depression, bogs formed. Receding glaciers frequently built a series of natural dams called moraines. Chains of lakes, so common in the Adirondacks, formed behind these moraines.

Hence, the stage upon which the dynamic drama of life in the Adirondacks is played has three principal parts. The hard platform floor keeps the waters on or near the land surface. The geological processes which made this region have provided channels through which the waters may drain off. The last Ice Age made this drainage difficult, so much water remains.

The hard metamorphic rock breaks down slowly. The soils are shallow because of this. As grades increase on mountainsides, the effects of erosion become more pronounced. Soil thickness becomes very thin. Heavy rains may saturate this soil. Landslides may then carry soil, trees, and everything else into the valleys.

It is on this thin mountain soil that man builds his trails. Newcomers frequently wonder why these trails often seem to go up stream beds. They don't realize that these "trail" streams came *after* man, not before him. His relentless walking has broken the soil and gravity has carried it away. Over the years the trails have become the low spots into which the surrounding waters descended. There is a lesson to be learned here. Always walk on rock where possible. Don't start that first depression that may become a stream bed in twenty years.

The kinds of plant life found in the Adirondacks are many. While the local environment will determine exactly which species will be found in a given area, Adirondack vegetation can be broadly grouped into five categories, referred to as site types: white pine, spruce swamp forest, mixed wood, hardwoods, and upper spruce slope sites. Characterized by a few readily identified trees, these sites tend to have specialized wildlife communities of plants and animals.

The white pine site type is generally found on sandy plains areas. It predominates from Lake Champlain to Glens Falls. White pines and other trees which have deep tap roots are most common. Mineral soils restrict what can survive there.

The spruce swamp site type is found wherever peaty or mucky soils occur in wet areas. If the swampy area has stagnant water, black spruces will be most common. If the water can flow easily, red spruce and balsam firs will be dominant.

The mixed woods begin above the swampy zones. The term "mixed woods" refers to the fact that both softwood and hardwood trees are found growing together in the same area. Soils are better and are slightly drier. Red maple, yellow birch, and hemlocks are most common. The softwoods decrease as elevations increase. The upper limit of this site type is reached where beeches begin to be seen.

Drainage is ideal on the lower mountain slopes. This is where the hardwood site type is found. The soils are very productive here. The primary trees are sugar maples and beech. However, yellow birch, black cherry, white ash, and other trees are found in lesser numbers.

Finally, at about 2500 ft. (765 m), the upper spruce slope site type begins. The red spruce and balsam fir again dominate. Tree size decreases as elevation increases. A timber line is reached if the mountain is high enough. The paper birch and mountain ash are the only hardwoods found in this site type, and they'll only be found at the lower limits of elevation.

Learn to identify these few trees and you'll better appreciate the forest you're traveling through on your outings. It's contagious. You'll soon be wondering why the ferns in the spruce swamp are different from those of the hardwoods. Why do the spring flowers linger longer on the trail edges than deeper in the forest? You'll begin to notice that bird species change as elevation and tree types change. Subtle but powerful biological interactions are set into motion by slight environmental variances. As you begin to notice them, your day's hiking destination won't seem quite as important. Each step will bring new opportunities for discovery.

What might you discover? One of the world's great moss collections is found in the Adirondacks clinging to wet cliffs and ledges. You might notice the great long, winding, glacial ridges called eskers. Huge white pines are often found growing on them. In the acidic bogs you may discover delicate sundew plants or thick waxy pitcher plants. Trees can also tell you much. The gradual reddening of the birch bark as you gain elevation gives clues as to how far you have yet to climb. When the hardwoods blend into the red spruce and balsam fir, you'll know that you're getting along on your climb. Paper birches at high elevations are signs of past forest fires. Mixed woods tell you how long it has been since the last lumbering. Why is it that the hemlocks, so common around Lake George, are found only in wind-protected vales in the high peaks?

Everything you see in the Adirondacks has an interesting history. Varying physical factors combine to form distinctive local environments. Organisms must adapt to these environments or perish. Everything affects everything else. Remember that you also affect everything else.

Think of the whole of the Adirondacks as you seek out the charms of the special places that will become "your" Adirondacks. Take time to observe that which surrounds you. Learn the story the land has to tell. It is the gift of the ages, and it began long before we appeared to sing its praises.

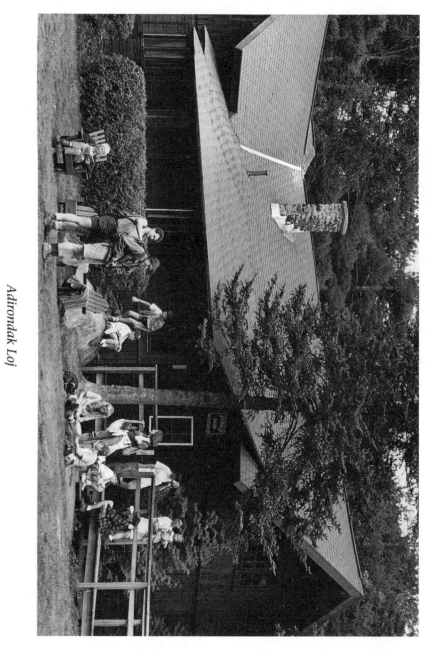

Adirondak Loj

Nancie Battaglia

The Adirondack Mountain Club

The Adirondack Mountain Club (ADK) is a nonprofit conservation, educa-tion, and recreation organization founded in 1922 for the purpose of protecting and enjoying the Forest Preserve of New York State. Organized into 26 chapters in two states, the Club's 35,000 members find experienced and knowledgeable persons on a local level to share common interests and concerns and almost any desired outdoor activity: hiking, backpacking, camping, canoeing, skiing, snowshoeing, and winter mountaineering. Its members also enjoy All-Club Outings and extended trips throughout the world.

ADK publishes guidebooks, maps, and other books relating to the natu-ral and social history of the Adirondacks. It also publishes educational bro-chures, and a magazine, *Adirondac*. Chapters publish their own newsletters as well, listing the hike schedules, monthly programs, and special activities of their local groups.

The Club sponsors outdoor skills workshops, natural history and educa-tional programs promoting the appreciation and careful use of New York's wild lands. Club volunteers and a professional trail crew carry out trail main-tenance throughout the High Peaks Region (some chapters also assume trail responsibility for areas outside the region) and administration of the Sum-mit Stewards program, which seeks to educate the public about the fragile alpine plans that grow on our highest peaks.

ADK operates two mountain lodges that serve as educational and recre-ational centers for Club members and the general public. Adirondak Loj, open all year, is a rustic, historic lodge eight miles south of Lake Placid on Heart Lake, on the site of Henry Van Hoevenberg's original turn-of-the-cen-tury log hotel. Loj accommodations include private and bunk rooms for forty-six persons. A separate rental cabin is available for groups of up to sixteen persons. Hearty meals are served family-style in the dining room. A lounge with fireplace offers a congenial atmosphere for after-dinner activities.

The Loj campgrounds, also open year round, have sixteen lean-tos, three "Canvas Cabins," and thirty-five campsites. Several lean-tos and campsites are open for winter camping, but sites for trailers and campers are usually inaccessible during snow months. The Club's High Peaks Information Cen-ter (HPIC) houses a large public room with educational displays, the latest backcountry information, and restrooms with hot showers. Its trading post offers last-minute camping and skiing supplies, trail snacks, and Adirondack-oriented publications.

In summer, a resident naturalist conducts seminars and programs and maintains a small nature museum. An outdoor amphitheater and several nature trails round out the Loj offerings. Ski and snowshoe rentals, guided tours, and skills instruction are available in the winter.

The Club also operates Johns Brook Lodge (JBL), a simple and informal complex 3½ miles by foot from the trailhead near Keene Valley. JBL provides an ideal base for hiking the Adirondack High Peaks Region. The main lodge is fully staffed from late June through Labor Day and can be used on a caretaker basis into October. The two out-buildings, Camp Peggy O'Brien and Grace Camp, have simple facilities where campers may cook their own meals and sleep in snug rooms year round. Campers using these facilities must supply their own sleeping equipment and pack in all necessary food and supplies. There are also three lean-tos available by reservation.

Because they adjoin state land, both the Loj and JBL afford convenient access to the high peaks (those 4000 ft. or over) and offer a wide choice of trails with a variety of lengths and degrees of difficulty.

At the southeastern corner of the park is the long log cabin that serves as ADK's Headquarters and Information Center. The building is located just off Exit 21 of the Northway (I-87), about 0.2 mi. south on Route 9N. It is open year-round, Monday–Saturday, 8:30 A.M.–5 P.M.

ADK staff at this facility provide information about hiking, canoeing, cross-country skiing, climbing and camping in the Adirondack Park. In addition, they host lectures, workshops, and exhibits; sell publications and ADK logo items; and provide membership information. ADK's public service programs are made possible by contributions to the organization and through member support. For further information, call or write ADK, 814 Goggins Road, Lake George, NY 12845-4117 (telephone: 518-668-4447).

Lake George and Southeast Section

An hour north of Albany and readily accessible by I-87 (Adirondack Northway) is the Lake George and Southeast section of the Adirondacks. Often bypassed by motorists, it is a region of open rocky summits and ridges offering unencumbered views and many interesting hiking and climbing opportunities. Where can one find a more compelling sight than Lake George surrounded by a quilt of multicolored leaves—reds, yellows, and purples of all descriptions—in autumn?

The Tongue Mountain Range forms a peninsula jutting out into Lake George. Its mountains are, from the north, Brown Mountain, Huckleberry Mountain, Five Mile Mountain, Fifth Peak, French Point Mountain, and First Peak. Across the lake stands Black Mountain, followed by Erebus Mountain, Buck Mountain and numerous smaller peaks.

It must be mentioned that rattlesnakes are occasionally seen on the Tongue Mountain Range and Black Mountain. The timber rattlesnake of New York State is a relatively shy creature. It will wish to avoid you even more than you wish to avoid it. These snakes are not likely to be seen along the hiking trails, though normal precautions should be taken. When climbing, take care where you put your hands on ledges. Examine the far side of logs before stepping over them. Be observant in sunny areas, where reptiles are likely to be found. Autumn hikers will find that these cold-blooded reptiles are usually far underground by the time the leaves have turned color.

The other mountains in this section stand out by themselves. Hadley Mountain is farthest south. It is a good mountain to climb in the spring, since its rocky trail has little of the mud so common at that time of year. Pharaoh Mountain, to the north, is reached by one of the many trails that abound in the region around Paradox Lake. Crane Mountain, to the west of Warrensburg, is a delightful climb.

THE TONGUE MOUNTAIN RANGE

The Tongue Mountain Range Trail has been broken up into three separate day trips. Experienced hikers may wish to combine them for longer outings. For instance, if two cars are available, you may wish to leave one at each end of the trail and hike through to Clay Meadows from the north end. The loop from Clay Meadows to Montcalm Point via French Pt. Mountain and back to Clay Meadows from Northwest Bay is a long 12.8 mi. (20.7 km). It should not be attempted by novices. There is no easy way out should an emergency occur. For experienced hikers, however, this is a tremendously rewarding circuit.

Access to the Tongue Mountain Range is via Rt. 9N. This route may be reached from Lake George Village or by exiting I-87 at Exit 24 and driving east to Rt. 9N. From the junction of the two roads, it is 4.7 mi. (7.5 km) farther north on Rt. 9N to Clay Meadows. This is 0.2 mi. (0.3 km) beyond the boat-launching site at Northwest Bay. The trailhead at the north end of the Tongue Mountain Range is another 4.5 mi. (7.2 km) north of Clay Meadows, just before the descent off Tongue Mountain begins. DEC signs mark each trailhead. There is parking available at each location.

1. Five Mile Mountain

Round-trip Time: 4 hrs. 30 min.
Round-trip Distance: 7.0 mi. (11.3 km)
Elevation Change: 1258 ft. (385 m)
Summit Elevation: 2258 ft. (691 m)
Difficulty: Easy for experienced hikers, moderate for novices.
Map: Silver Bay 7.5'; or Bolton Landing 15'

This is a good trip for beginners. Open views reward the climber for much of the way. The tired hiker can turn back at any point and still feel satisfied. There is no water on this route.

Use the northern end trailhead access. (See above.) A short distance from the start, the trail makes a sharp left turn off the fire road. There is a DEC register at this location. Continuing, the gently rising trail meets a yellow DEC-marked trail at a junction at 0.65 mi. (1.0 km). The yellow trail leads straight ahead 1.0 mi. (1.6 km). to a lookout at Deer Leap.

Following the blue markers, the main trail bears right, up a slight rise. Several lookouts appear as elevation is gained. Black Ledges is reached at 1.2 mi. (1.0 km). The rocks to the left front offer excellent viewing. Mother Bunch Islands are seen in the lake below and Black Mountain rises to the east. After leaving Black Ledges, you shortly arrive at the summit of Brown Mountain.

A careful observer may be able to see Northwest Bay through the trees to the right. Following open ledges and woods, you reach Tongue Mountain lean-to at 2.6 mi. (4.2 km). It makes a nice resting place. The lichen and flowers found growing on the open rock slopes around the lean-to are fascinating to study or to photograph. Walk on the bare rock as much as possible to protect this vegetation. From the lean-to, marvelous vistas of the Adirondack High Peaks spread out before you to the northwest.

The trail follows rock cairns and blue painted arrows over rock to the right rear of the lean-to. Easy grades lead another 0.7 mi. (1.1 km) over Huckleberry Mountain to a sign in an open spot. Only the remains of a fireplace indicate there was once another lean-to at this location.

The top of Five Mile Mountain is gained at 3.5 mi. (5.7 km). It offers good views of Black Mountain and, beyond it to the northeast, the Green Mountains of Vermont. Outstanding views can be found on the downslopes of the mountain farther to the south.

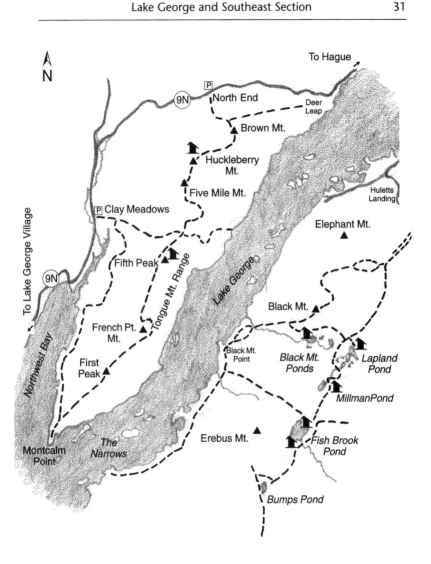

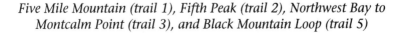

Five Mile Mountain (trail 1), Fifth Peak (trail 2), Northwest Bay to Montcalm Point (trail 3), and Black Mountain Loop (trail 5)

If a second car has been left at Clay Meadows, it is possible to continue to the four-way junction in the col 1.65 mi. (2.7 km) farther along the trail. It is another 1.95 mi. (3.2 km) to Clay Meadows. This would make a loop totaling 7.1 mi. (11.5 km). There is an 800-ft. (245 m) drop in elevation on a steep trail from Brown Mountain to the junction.

The trail from the north end of Tongue Mountain to the summit of Brown Mountain is also an excellent snowshoeing route.

2. Fifth Peak

Round-trip Time: 3 hrs. 30 min.
Round-trip Distance: 5.4 mi. (8.6 km)
Elevation Change: 1350 ft. (413 m)
Summit Elevation: 1770 ft. (541 m)
Difficulty: Generally easy but steady climbing.
Map: Silver Bay 7.5' and Shelving Rock 7.5'; or Bolton Landing 15'

Parking is found on the east side of Rt. 9N, just north of Clay Meadows. (See p. 27–28.) From the trailhead follow blue DEC markers on a level, and then gradually descending, trail.

You pass through a stand of white pine where interesting ground cover can be seen. A trail junction is reached at 0.4 mi. (0.6 km). Continue straight ahead, now following red trail markers. The tote road now begins to rise at a moderately steep grade through a mixed-wood forest. A cascading brook is crossed on an old bridge.

After five minutes the trail becomes more rocky. Watch for where the trail makes a sharp left and then a sharp right turn. The path then levels. For a while it becomes a pleasant stroll. Gradual climbing begins again at two switchbacks. Downed branches may obscure trail markers in this short section; keep a sharp eye out. A spring is passed on the left as the trail swings upward to the right.

At 1.95 mi. (3.2 km) is a four-way junction. The red trail continues straight ahead, where it eventually descends to Five Mile Point on Lake George far below. The trail left goes 1.7 mi. (2.7 km) to the summit of Five Mile Mountain.

Follow the blue trail, right, for Fifth Peak. Another 0.55 mi. (0.9 km) farther on, a small sign at a trail junction indicates a side trail to the left. Fifth Peak is 1500 ft. (459 m) along this side trail. A curving path leads you to a lean-to and the marvelous vantage point beyond.

What a magnificent view awaits you. Green islands, like emeralds, glitter below in the deep blue lake. From the grassy lookout, Black, Erebus, and Elephant mountains stand out across the lake. To the south, French Pt. Mountain is prominent.

The Mohawks called the beautiful body of water you are looking at *Andia-to-roc-tee* (place where the lake contracts). Father Isaac Jogues, returning in 1646, christened it Lac Du St. Sacrament (Lake of the Blessed Sacrament). General William Johnson gave the lake its present name, Lake George, in commemoration of King George II.

The delicate appearance of this region reminds one more of the Catskills than the high peaks of the Adirondacks. Hemlocks and white pines are found instead of the expected red spruce and balsam fir. Ground cover and open grassy slopes grace the ridges. The windswept upper reaches provide continuously changing scenes as you hike along.

3. Northwest Bay to Montcalm Point

Round-trip Time: 4 hrs. 30 min.
Round-trip Distance: 10.8 mi. (17.5 km)
Elevation Change: 190 ft. (58 m)
Difficulty: Easy; a long gradual upgrade is found near the end of the return trip.
Map: Silver Bay 7.5', Shelving Rock 7.5', Bolton Landing 7.5; or Bolton Landing 15'

This is a beautiful ramble along an old tote road to Montcalm Point. Fully two-thirds of the trip is along the shoreline of Northwest Bay.

Starting at Clay Meadows (see p. 27–28), the trail leads off to the east, following blue markers. Gradually descending, it crosses a swampy stream on a long corduroy bridge.

Keep alert for the abrupt turn to the right that the trail takes at 0.4 mi. (0.6 km). A red trail continues straight ahead; your trail swings to the right down a bank. The steady drop in elevation seems nice, but it may appear to be much longer on the return trip.

The variety of plant and animal life makes this an interesting walk. A stream and a marsh are passed. On higher, drier ground the trail parallels the inlet to Northwest Bay for some time. Birdlife abounds here and large waterbirds are commonly seen.

Lacy hemlocks cloak the shoreline. Old axe blazes mark the original route. The path follows the water's edge, occasionally climbing to avoid obstacles but soon returning to the crystalline water. A few streams and one very attractive little waterfall beckon you along the way.

At 5.0 mi. (8.1 km), a trail jct. is reached. The blue trail markers lead left into the Tongue Mountain Range and begin to ascend the ridge toward First Peak and French Point Mountains. Proceed straight ahead to the Point.

Montcalm Point is named after the Marquis de Montcalm. His large military force laid siege to Ft. William Henry during the French and Indian Wars. James Fenimore Cooper's *Last of the Mohicans* made this event forever famous. Montcalm was never able to adequately explain why his forces permitted their Indian allies to massacre hundreds of surrendering men, women, and children on that grizzly morning in August of 1757.

From the point, the Narrows of Lake George are seen to the north. Across the lake is Shelving Rock. Erebus Mountain is seen to the north, on the east side of the lake. Buck Mountain rises to the right of Shelving Rock.

4. Buck Mountain

Round-trip Time: 4 to 5 hrs.
Round-trip Distance: 6.6 mi. (10.7 km)
Elevation Change: 1990 ft. (609 m)
Summit Elevation: 2334 ft. (714 m)
Difficulty: Moderately strenuous, in part, with some steep sections.
Map: Bolton Landing 7.5' and Shelving Rock 7.5; or Bolton
  Landing 15'

Buck Mountain offers splendid views of the Lake George mountains and the Adirondack peaks far beyond to the north. Unique, however, is the sight sometimes seen from this bald peak when you gaze down at the water below. Dozens of small sailing craft on a sunny summer weekend form ever-changing patterns as sailors exhibit their skills. The spectacle is not soon forgotten.

Access to the trailhead is best gained from the Adirondack Northway (I-87) at Exit 20. Follow Rt. 9 northward a short distance and turn right onto Rt. 149. This is the road to Whitehall. Just past a golf course on the left, turn left onto Rt. 9L. Follow this northward until you come to the right-hand turn for Pilot Knob and Kattskill Bay. This is Pilot Knob Road. Follow it 3.5 mi. (5.6 km) until you see the large DEC sign and parking area on the right for Buck Mountain.

The trail starts from a trail register at the rear of the parking area. Running a flat course over a wide woods road, it occasionally passes side paths, until a creek is crossed at 0.2 mi. (0.3 km). A junction is reached soon thereafter, and the Buck Mt. Trail turns sharply left. **Watch for this turn.** Yellow trail markers can be seen from this point and should be followed to the summit.

After a few winding turns, the trail ascends a long moderate grade. Attractive Butternut Brook is seen below, as your route climbs higher and higher above it. In summer, scents of the mixed wood forest awaken your senses. Rock outcrops above you at left are interesting. One immense boulder seen along the trail looks like a super loaf of bread.

A second stream is crossed and at 1.2 mi. (1.9 km) a junction is reached. The trail right leads 3.1 mi. (5.0 km) to Inman Pond and 2.8 mi. (4.5 km) to the Lower Hogtown parking area.

The Buck Mountain trail curves upward to the left, reaching a gushing stream in a few minutes. Years ago, a long pipe protruded from the stream here and hikers paused for a refreshing drink. The route gradually changes from a woods road to a path. Avoid the side trail to the right that soon appears.

The first substantial steep grade is soon surmounted, and gradual grades

The Narrows of Lake George

Lawrence King

are again the norm. The trail curves left as a wet area is passed. A second and much longer steep grade brings you to the first lookout, on the right from which Crossett Pond is seen to the east.

Walking is now level for about ten minutes. As the grade steepens moderately, you break out on the open rock; views to the west and south begin to appear. Following yellow paint blazes ever upward, increasingly more interesting scenes appear around you.

Delicate vegetation of the open rock is easily destroyed. Walk on bare rock where possible and don't stray from the trail. Protect this fragile biota.

Still moving upward, the trail drops into a small rock depression and a trail junction is reached. The trail to the right leads on another 2.2 mi. (3.5 km) to Shelving Rock Rd. Continuing to the left front, the Buck Mountain route leads generally northwest over bare rock to a magnificent outlook just past the high point of rock.

In summer, sailboats flitter about below like water bugs. Crane Mountain is to the west. Prospect Mountain can be seen to the southeast. Across the lake to the north is the Tongue Mountain Range and Northwest Bay. Beyond them stretches the panorama of Adirondack high peaks. Up the lake on the east shore are Erebus Mountain and Black Mountain with its tower just visible. Directly below is Pilot Knob.

As you look downward to the northwest over Little Buck Mountain toward Shelving Rock, it is easy to see why this whole open rock expanse was once called "the deer pasture."

5. Black Mountain Loop

Round-trip Time: 4 hrs.
Round-trip Distance: 6.7 mi. (10.7 km)
Elevation Change: 1046 ft. (319 m)
Summit Elevation: 2646 ft. (809 m)
Difficulty: Easy climbing, with occasional steepness.
Map: Shelving Rock 7.5'; or Bolton Landing 15'

"A sentinel, it seems, overlooking the whole lake and mountains round about, the first to welcome the rising sun, and at evening, glowing in the splendor of the dying day, while the valleys below are misty with the shadows of the coming night." This is how Seneca Ray Stoddard described Black Mountain in 1890 in *Lake George and Lake Champlain*. He was right. The highest mountain on the shores of Lake George, it provides an unsurpassed panorama of both the lake and the Adirondacks to the west.

Access to the trailhead is off Rt. 22, north of Whitehall. Approximately 4.5 mi. (7.3 km) north of where Rt. 22 crosses Lake Champlain is a sign for Hulett's Landing. Turn left and proceed 2.7 mi. (4.4 km) to Pike Brook Road. Turn left and travel another 0.8 mi. (1.3 km) along Pike Brook Road. As you begin to descend a hill, the large DEC sign and parking area is seen on the right. This is 3.5 mi. (5.6 km) from Rt. 22.

The trail leads up a slope a short distance to a woods road. Turn left and follow this road 0.5 mi. (0.8 km) to a trail junction just before a private home. From this point the fire tower on top of Black Mountain can be seen. The trail leaves the road to the right and skirts the private property. Do not stray off the trail at this point.

The small red DEC trail markers should be followed. A snowmobile trail with large orange markers winds in and out of the hiking trail. Be sure to follow the smaller trail markers.

The wide woods road you are now following continues gradually upward. A sign soon indicates a side trail left to Lapland Pond. Pass it, and continue straight ahead. Follow the hiking trail markers closely in this area because a snowmobile trail intersects yet again.

Soon the trail again begins to climb gently. A spring is passed on the right. A rushing brook is soon crossed. The woods road terminates and the trail becomes a footpath. Surmounting a rocky slope, it levels somewhat before winding its way up to the fire observer's cabin and fire tower.

The sight from the summit will long be remembered. The Narrows of Lake George are below you. The Tongue Mountain Range stretches out along the opposite shoreline. Mt. Marcy and other High Peaks are seen in the far distance. Elephant Mountain is to the north and Erebus Mountain is to the south. The Green Mountains of Vermont are seen to the east, beyond the southern part of Lake Champlain. Note the color difference between Lake George and this section of Lake Champlain.

If you were to return by the same route, the round-trip distance would be 5.0 mi. (8.1 km). The loop trail provides a much more interesting journey, however.

The trail drops off the west side of the mountain and leads 1.3 mi. (2.1 km) to Black Mountain Pond. This trail descends rapidly with several switchbacks. Outstanding vantage points offer excellent views of the lake below.

Near the base of the mountain you reach a trail junction. Turn left and follow yellow trail markers past Black Mountain Pond and then Round Pond. There is a lean-to at the first pond.

As you leave this area, the snowmobile trail is seen again, coming in from the right. Your trail leads straight on, up a small grade. Yellow markers take you onward for another twenty minutes. Keep your eyes on the markers in this section. You will reach Lapland Pond junction. You are now 2.2 mi. (3.6 km) from your starting point.

Turning left from this junction, follow blue markers. The trail soon becomes a woods road again. It is generally level. Eventually you will arrive at a beautiful brook with a bridge over it. Its cooling waters provide a much appreciated respite. A slight grade brings you to the road back to the parking area. Turn right here. It is a little under a mile back to the trail origin.

6. Hadley Mountain
Round-trip Time: 3 hrs.
Round-trip Distance: 3.6 mi. (5.8 km)
Elevation Change: 1526 ft. (467 m)
Summit Elevation: 2675 ft. (818 m)
Difficulty: Easy, but climbs steadily for the first 1.5 mi. (2.4 km).
Map: Conklingville 7.5'; or Lake Luzerne 15'

Hadley Mountain is a good mountain to take youngsters up since the grade, though steady, is not difficult. The view will certainly make them want to continue hiking. It is also a totally enjoyable mountain to snowshoe on.

Access to the mountain is from the village of Hadley, best reached from the east on Rt. 9N to Lake Luzerne village. Then cross the Hudson River to Hadley via Church, Main, and Bridge streets. If coming from the west, around the Great Sacandaga Lake, follow the Conklingville Road. In Hadley, turn onto Stony Creek Road. Drive north about 3 mi. (4.9 km) until you come to the marked Hadley Hill Road on the left. Proceed along the Hadley Hill Road a little over 4 mi. (6.5 km) until you come to Tower Road. There is a small sign on the right side of the road. This is the second major right-hand turn along Hadley Hill Road. This road descends a long grade for another 1.5 mi. (2.4 km) to the Hadley Mountain trailhead. It is on the left and is marked by a sign. Parking for several cars is available in the summer. In the winter, it will be necessary to squeeze your car to the side of the road so other cars can pass.

The trail up the mountain follows the old jeep trail to the fire observer's cabin for most of the way to summit. Use of a vehicle was a destructive practice that left an eroded, rutted trail for hikers. However, excellent trail improvement projects by ADK trail crews have again made this a very pleasant ascent. The mountain is a fine beginner's climb for both young and old.

The red DEC-marked trail starts up through a nice hemlock stand. The steady, easy-to-moderate grade continues for 1.0 mi. (1.6 km) until the top of West Mountain Ridge is reached. The mixed-wood forest trail is interspersed with glacial boulders, small cliffs, and other features. It is an interesting walk.

Once on the ridge top, the trail turns to the right, heading northwest. The last 0.8 mi. (1.3 km) is very open. Superior views make this a pleasant stroll. As the trail curves around the ridge below the fire tower, new vistas continually present themselves to the climber.

The summit is almost entirely open. It is not necessary to climb the tower. The Great Sacandaga Lake is due south. On a clear day the Helderbergs and Catskills can be seen beyond the lake. Some high peaks can be seen to the north from the tower. The Green Mountains of Vermont are to the east. Spruce Mountain is to the west. You'll want to spend a long time on the top. Walks along the ridge to the north are quite enjoyable.

7. *Crane Mountain*

Round-trip Time: 4 hrs.
Round-trip Distance: 7.4 mi. (12.0 km)
Elevation Change: 1154 ft. (353 m)
Summit Elevation: 3254 ft. (995 m)
Difficulty: The middle section is quite steep, but most of the rest is easy.
Map: Johnsburg 7.5'; or North Creek 15'

This rocky summit provides some stiff climbing but is well worth it. The best way to approach the mountain is by the Wevertown-Johnsburg-Thurman route. From Wevertown on Rt. 28, drive 2.0 mi. (3.2 km) southwest on Rt. 8 to Johnsburg. At Johnsburg turn south onto South Johnsburg Road and proceed 6 mi. (9.6 km) to a T intersection at Thurman. There is a small Crane Mountain sign at this intersection. Turn right onto Garnet Lake Road. Follow this road 1.5 mi. (2.4 km) to where a second, but smaller, Crane Mountain sign indicates another right-hand turn. Travel this good gravel road approximately 2.0 mi. (3.2 km) until it ends at a small parking area at the trailhead. The last half mile (0.8 km) of this road narrows considerably; drive carefully.

The trailhead begins at the road end and a DEC register is seen soon after. There are two trails up the mountain from this point. A short, very steep, trail leads straight ahead from the register. The trail to the left is long but far more interesting. It is this second route that is described here.

From the register, take the fork left along a level track. At 0.4 mi. (0.6 km), this path widens as it merges with an old abandoned woods road. Bearing right, this delightful lane leads after another rolling mile (1.6 km) to a marked intersection near the old Putnam Farm.

Turn right. Soon after this section begins, a natural bridge is crossed. On a hot day the cool breezes emanating from the stream channel's tunnel are very refreshing. Beyond the bridge, one begins a gradual climb that greatly steepens as it approaches Crane Mt. Pond.

In the 0.9 mi. (1.5 km) from the Putnam Farm intersection to Crane Pond Outlet, the trail gains some 900 ft.(275 m) in elevation. Views begin to open up and the rocky path requires your attention.

Turn right at Crane Mt. Pond Outlet and follow the shoreline. The summit can be seen across the water. At one time the fire observer's cabin was located at this pond's edge. Avoid the cross-over trail to the other summit trail that comes in from the right. Instead, continue around the shoreline to the north. The trail eventually swings away from the pond's perimeter path. After climbing up through the woods, you'll reach a rocky ridge in about 15 minutes. The open ridge trail winds southeastward to where the fire tower once stood and offers several outlooks.

Hadley, Blue, Baldhead, and Moose mountains are seen to the south. Indian Lake and Snowy Mountain are off to the northwest. Crane Mountain Pond dominates the view to the west. The return trip might well

View from summit of Crane Mountain

Gail Pfau

include a cooling swim in this refreshing body of water.

A shorter, alternate descent to the trailhead is possible by traveling a short distance eastward along the ridge. If you can negotiate the nearly vertical drop on a suspended ladder at the onset, you'll find the rest of this route less rigorous. It is, however, challenging enough to keep your attention.

8. Pharaoh Mountain

Round-trip Time: 4 hrs. 30 min.
Round-trip Distance: 9.3 mi. (15.1 km)
Elevation Change: 1257 ft. (384 m)
Summit Elevation: 2557 ft. (782 m)
Difficulty: Easy for experienced hikers, challenging for novices.
Map: Pharaoh Mountain 7.5'; or Paradox Lake 15'

From the Adirondack Northway (I-87), take Exit 28. Follow Rt. 74 east a short distance to Rt. 9 and turn right (south). One-half mile (0.8 km) down Rt. 9, turn left onto Alder Meadow Road. This road is about 2.0 mi. (3.2 km) north of Schroon Lake Village.

Keep on this road for 2.2 mi. (3.5 km); at that point, bear left at the fork in the road. Travel another 1.4 mi. (2.2 km) to a parking area at the end. The road is open to the parking area year round. It is a 9.3 mi. (15.1 km) round trip to the summit of Pharaoh Mountain from this point.

Crane Pond Road leads out of the right side of this parking area and runs 1.9 mi. to a parking area near Crane Pond. Currently (1996) it is legal to drive over this road. A committee has been appointed by the N.Y.S. governor to study this and other roads that penetrate areas designated as wilderness.

The trailhead is at the end of the parking area, where a register is located. Heading southwest from the register, over a large flat boulder, follow red markers. The outlet of Crane Pond is immediately crossed on a log bridge. The wide trail proceeds over rolling terrain. The mixed woods of hemlock, birch, and beech are particularly beautiful in autumn.

At 0.7 mi. (1.1 km) a trail junction is reached. The Pharaoh Mountain trail makes a sharp right and then a sharp left. Climbing a short rise, you see Glidden Marsh below to the left. This is one of several trout-stocked waters in this region.

A series of gradual rises indicates that you have reached the lower slopes of the mountain. From this point onward, the grades become progressively steeper and longer.

When stopping to rest, look at the rock that makes up this mountain. It is basically a metamorphic gneiss formed from the original granite of the area. Note the alternating bands of light and dark-colored minerals in the rock. There is great variation throughout the mountain, giving clues to what was happening in this area many millions of years ago. The reddish mineral is garnet.

The course of the former telephone line to the tower crosses the trail in several places. Follow the marked trail; it is safer. As you reach the upper third of the mountain, you'll notice the route is mostly over bare rock. When the first good open view, to the west, appears at a rocky shelf to the right, you'll know you are close to the top. One last steep climb, through a grassy area, will bring you to the fire observer's cabin. The tower supports are still present, but the tower has been removed.

The clear, rocky summit is a good place for a leisurely lunch topped off, in season, with the blueberries that appear here. At least three bench markers and one Verplanck Colvin survey marker can be located near the fire tower. Colvin was responsible for the early surveys of the Adirondacks. His enthusiasm and wisdom played a major part in the establishment of the Adirondack Park. Survey control points on Pharaoh Mountain were used as early as 1878.

Schroon Lake is seen to the west with Spectacle Pond, Desolate Brook, and other smaller bodies of water somewhat closer. A short walk to the southwest brings you to another vantage point from which Pharaoh Lake is seen at the base of the mountain. Treadway Mountain is to the east.

This is an excellent area for snowshoeing and skiing in winter.

Indian Lake and South Section

This section might be called the forgotten part of the Adirondacks. Though few mountains of any great size can be found, good views can be had from those that exist. It is a region of rolling forest, small lakes, and quiet marshes. There is a difference here. You can be alone. In fact, on some trails in this area you might be surprised to meet another person.

This is the land of Nick Stoner and French Louie, legendary woodsmen of yesteryear. Coyotes still abound, and first-time campers have been known to sit bolt upright in their sleeping bags when a loon screamed in the night.

It is good snowshoeing country. Cross-country skiers all have their favorite spots. Hunters come in season, but for the most part the hiker seeking solitude can find it.

The trips described here are easily reached by car. Rts. 8, 10 and 30 provide access into this section.

9. Snowy Mountain
Round-trip Time: 5 hrs.
Round-trip Distance: 7.5 mi. (12.2 km)
Elevation Change: 2105 ft. (644 m)
Summit Elevation: 3899 ft. (1192 m)
Difficulty: Challenging. Long hike, steep much of the way, fatiguing if
    not in good condition.
Maps: Indian Lake 7.5'; or Indian Lake 15'; or Indian Lake metric

Through a joint venture with the DEC and town of Indian Lake, the Adirondack Mountain Club's trail crew greatly improved the condition of the Snowy Mountain Trail in the summer of 1987.

Snowy Mountain just misses being in the 4000-ft. (1233 m) class by a few feet. The vertical climb is actually greater than many of the 46'er peaks, since the base is at a lower elevation.

The mountain is located on the west side of Indian Lake along Rt. 30. It is 7.3 mi. (11.7 km) south of Indian Lake village and 4.7 mi. (7.6 km) north of Lewey Lake Outlet and the boat-launching site. Along the west side of the road, the trailhead for Snowy Mountain climbs a bank. A large paved area is available for parking several cars on the opposite side of the highway.

The trail heads westward up Beaver Brook Valley, following red markers. Generally flat or rolling, it crosses several small streams. Finally, after being within hearing of Beaver Brook down to the right for some time, the path leads below to the rock-bordered stream and crosses it at 1.2 mi. (1.9 km).

A steep climb for a short distance moves you off the valley floor. From this point on, however, the previously closed-in trail opens up and is more pleasant. You may have noticed that the largest trees are sugar maples and old spruces. Beaver Brook is again crossed at 1.9 mi. (3.1 km) and young spruces are seen beginning to emerge beneath the branches of the older trees. This is the sign of a climax forest.

Occasional hunting trails branch off, but the main trail is obvious. The route crosses from the right bank of the brook to the left bank. A 2.5 mi. (4.1 km) a tributary is crossed and you begin a long, steady climb up the mountain. The soil thins and is drier. As a result, the trees now become much smaller in diameter.

Gradually the trail becomes rockier. A good lookout to the rear is found at 3.2 mi. (5.2 km). The reconditioned trail is extremely steep for the remainder of the way to the summit. The site of the former observer's cabin is reached at 3.8 mi. (6.2 km). A large cliff edge provides a fine view eastward to Indian Lake and beyond. This makes a good place for a lunch break. There is a small spring at wood's edge, near the place where the trail continues to the tower, but its quality varies since the fire observer is no longer here to maintain it.

The summit is only 500 ft. (153 m) up a gentle grade to the southwest. Unfortunately, the tower is no longer open for viewing. A trail southeast of the tower leads to an unusual lookout point where cliffs drop off several hundred feet. Another side trail takes you 50 yds. (46 m) west of the spring to a lookout where Buell and Panther mountains can be seen. The vista down to the ponds along Squaw Brook from this place is exquisite. From the fire observer's cabin, it is possible to see Mount Marcy and the high peaks to the north.

10. Echo Cliffs at Panther Mountain

Round-trip Time: 1 hr. 30 min.
Round-trip Distance: 1.7 mi. (2.7 km)
Elevation Change: 680 ft. (207 m)
Summit Elevation: 2425 ft. (742 m)
Difficulty: Easy, with some steepness near terminus.
Maps: Piseco Lake 7.5'; or Piseco Lake 15'; or Piseco Lake metric

Echo Cliffs at Panther Mountain offer a nice little climb and a surprisingly good view of Piseco Lake and areas to the east.

Access to the trailhead is from the West Shore Road along Piseco Lake. West Shore Road is off Rt. 8, 2.9 mi. (4.7 km) south of where Rt. 8 meets Rt. 10. Drive along West Shore Road 2.6 mi. (4.2 km) from Rt. 8. At this point, a small DEC sign marks the trailhead. There is parking on the opposite side of the road.

The trailhead sign indicates an ascent of 1048 ft. (320 m). This is the vertical distance to the summit, not to Echo Cliffs. Following blue DEC markers, the trail leads through a mature maple-beech forest.

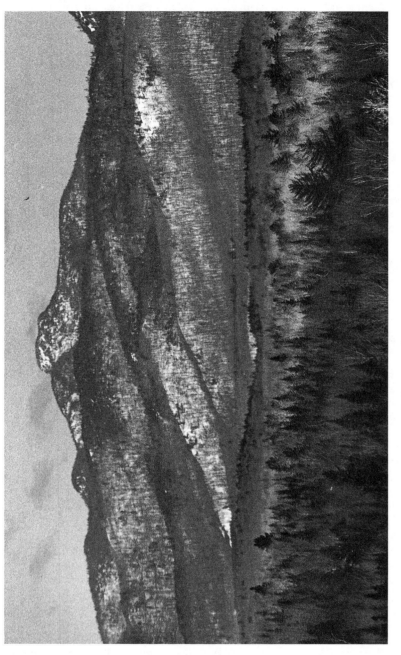

Winter on Snowy Mountain

R. Meyer

Varying grades provide relatively easy walking for the first 0.6 mi. (1.0 km), until a large boulder is reached. At this point, the way becomes more rocky and consistently steeper. Five minutes later, a large rock outcrop is passed. Soon after, the trail becomes rather steep for the short remaining distance to Echo Cliffs. Red spruce are now present, giving evidence of higher elevation.

The splendid view is to the southeast. Higgins Bay and Spy Lake are seen to the left front. Beyond Spy Lake, Three Sisters Mountains are seen. To the left is the huge bulk of Hamilton Mountain. A small portion of Oxbow Lake can be seen to the northeast. The long, narrow, curved body of water to the right front beyond Piseco Lake is Big Bay.

Panther Mountain got its name, back in time, when $20 was paid for a "painter" pelt and $10 for a "whelp." There is currently some interest in trying to reestablish this needed predator inside the Adirondack Park. By culling the old and sick, this native cat might strengthen the deer population in this region.

11. Chimney Mountain
Round-trip Time: 2 hrs. 30 min.
Round-trip Distance: 3 mi. (4.9 km)
Elevation Change: 874 ft. (266 m)
Difficulty: A fairly rugged climb, but short.
Maps: Bullhead Mountain 7.5'; or Thirteenth Lake 15';
    or Thirteenth Lake metric

Chimney Mt. is geologically unique. The "chimney" is a bulwark of interesting stone. In places, caves lead into its depths. Its tectonic history has yet to be fully understood. For the day hiker, this little peak is full of surprises and is a splendid short outing.

Trail access is near Kings Flow. Drive south 0.6 mi. (1.0 km) on NY 30 from its intersection with NY 28 in the village of Indian Lake. Then bear left onto Big Brook Rd. and travel 1.2 mi. (1.9 km) to where a causeway crosses Lake Abanakee. Continue another 2.1 mi. (3.4 km) to the intersection with Hutchins and Moulton Roads. Big Brook Rd. turns right. It is another 5.6 mi. (9.0 km) to Chimney Mt. Wilderness Lodge and the road's end at Kings Flow. There is a specified parking area for hikers' vehicles and a small day-use parking fee.

From the parking area, walk east a short distance on a dirt road to a DEC sign post. Bear left from it to another sign post, which is the Chimney Mt. trailhead. Blue DEC trail markers guide you into this interesting deciduous forest. Easy walking eventually brings you to a trail register at 0.4 mi. (0.6 km). From here, the trail crosses a brook and begins to ascend several moderate grades. These will steepen progressively. The trail grade lessens briefly at 0.7 mi. (1.1 km), but soon you return to steep climbing.

There is a trail junction at 1.1 mi. (1.8 km) and a nice lookout to the west over Kings Flow and Round Pond. (The path to the left at this junction circles to a low ridge opposite the chimney. It has a viewing point. If you desire still more hiking on your descent, you may wish to explore this area.) Continuing on the main trail, you climb a steep rock massif before reaching an open spot at 1.2 mi. (1.9 km). Clear views are to the south and Bullhead Mt. is northeast.

The trail dips slightly before the final rocky ascent to the base of the chimney. Passing through a narrow passageway brings you to a high rock enclosure. Ahead, the trail dips again. A little more walking brings you to the trail's end at the large chimney-like formation that gives the mountain its name. Its structure begs explanation. The intricate assemblage of rock rises skyward in wild array. Few enthusiasts choose to climb to its top and ascent is not encouraged. Only experienced technical rock climbers should attempt it.

The elevation here is 2609 ft. (795 m). The mountain's true summit is seldom climbed. It is reached by a rugged bushwhack to the east. Summit elevation is 2711 ft. (826 m). The flat topped mountain northward on the horizon to the left of the chimney is Blue Mountain.

12. Wilcox Lake Walk
Round-trip Time: 5 hrs. 30 mins.
Round-trip Distance: 10.1 mi. (16.2 km)
Elevation Change: 480 ft. (147 m)
Difficulty: Easy walking, but a long trip.
Maps: Hope Falls 7.5'; or Harrisburg 15'; or Harrisburg metric

The hike from Brownell's Camp to Wilcox Lake is a woodland ramble at its very best. It follows an old tote road through a magnificent mixed-wood forest. Over half of the trip is along East Stony Creek.

Access to the trail is off Rt. 30, above the Great Sacandaga Lake, on the southern edge of the hamlet of Hope. At 3.2 mi. (5.2 km) north of the Benson Section signpost for the Northville-Placid Trail, turn right on Creek Road. There is a family cemetery plot at this intersection.

Proceed along Creek Road for 2.8 mi. (4.5 km) until a Y-intersection with DEC signs is reached. Turn left onto Hope Falls Road. At its midpoint it will become a dirt road. Proceed along this road 4.9 mi. (7.9 km) to a DEC signpost at the trailhead, along East Stony Creek. Park off the road as much as possible. Do not proceed onto the Brownell Camp property, which is private.

Following orange DEC snowmobile markers and periodic blue DEC markers, you will cross Tenant Creek on a wooden bridge in about ten minutes. The trail is an old logging route through a pretty, mixed-wood forest. After about a mile of walking, you return to the banks of East Stony Creek.

Turning right, the woods road parallels the stream going upstream for close to 3 mi. (9.9 km). In the spring the water is high and fast-moving. Its

The chimney on Chimney Mountain

R. Meyer

rocks, sparkling reflections, and ever-changing scenes make it fascinating. In season many flowers are found along the stream banks.

Occasional tributaries are crossed. At one point, the old trail rises far up the bank until it is a considerable distance from the shimmering water below. Some time later you begin the descent to Dayton Creek (3.5 mi.). After crossing Dayton Creek, the trail parallels the stream until, at 4.1 mi., it meets the junction to Harrisburg Lake and the metal suspension bridge crossing East Stony Creek.

Turning left, cross the suspension bridge and begin the last 1.0 mi. (1.6 km) climb over the low shoulder of Wilcox Mountain to Wilcox Lake. Follow the large orange snowmobile trail markers and occasional yellow DEC trail markers carefully in this short section. Switchbacks take you up the steady but moderate slope.

Near the top of the grade, a T junction is found. The left turn leads 4.5 mi. (7.3 km) to Willis Lake.

Bear right for the last 0.3 mi. (0.5 km) down the slope to Wilcox Lake. You soon come to the jeep trail, which enters from the right. Continue straight ahead to the DEC register found at the lake's edge.

The lake is good-sized and has good fishing. As you look around this handsome lake, consider that it cost "tenderfeet" $9.00 a week to stay at the Brownell Camp's woods hotel back in 1917. They came by smoky train and dusty stagecoach to spend a season in these climes. You'll probably be home in a nice soft bed tonight, having made the return drive in a few hours.

13. Cod Pond

Round-trip Time: 1 hr. 30 min.
Round-trip Distance: 2.2 mi. (3.5 km)
Elevation Change: 195 ft. (59 m)
Difficulty: Easy
Maps: South Mountain 7.5'

Cod Pond is a pleasant walk through a hardwood forest and is host to an abundance of birds and other wildlife. The trailhead is located along Rt. 8, 9.5 mi. (15.2 km) north of the Rt. 30 intersection near Wells and 15.5 mi. (24.8 km) south of the Rt. 8 junction with Rt. 28 in Wevertown. There is a small trailhead parking area on the east side of the road, adjacent to the Stewart Creek bridge. Though many are old and faded, orange markers appear frequently along the trail, indicating its use by snowmobilers in winter. From a gate in the parking area, the trail begins a gradual ascent into a hardwood forest. However, within 400 ft., and for the next 0.2 mi. (0.3 km), the forest canopy opens to reveal an area heavily damaged by the July 1995 microburst storm that cut a large path of blowdown through portions of the Adirondacks. It is remarkable to see how the area is making a comeback after such a dramatic event.

Within this section, the trail to Cod Pond makes a right turn at the junction with the North Bend and Baldwin Spring trail. Soon after, the trail leaves the microburst-damaged area and continues its gradual climb, bearing to the left when it meets up with the snowmobile trail to Cotter Brook on the right (0.3 mi.). At 0.5 mi. (0.8 km) the trail begins a gentle descent before climbing up onto a ridge where, at 1.0 mi. (1.6 km), Cod Pond is visible through the trees to the left. Soon, the trail passes a designated camping area on the right and within another 150 ft. (45 m) leads to the shore of Cod Pond. This is a beautiful spot to picnic and listen to the wind in the trees.

14. Sawyer Mountain
Round-trip Time: 2 hrs.
Round-trip Distance: 2.3 mi. (3.7 km)
Elevation Change: 650 ft. (199 m)
Summit Elevation: 2610 ft. (798 m)
Difficulty: Easy.
Maps: Rock Lake 7.5'; or Blue Mountain 15'; or Blue Mountain metric

Sawyer Mountain is an easy climb. The trail leads up through a mature forest of maple and beech to the lookout, just past the summit. For such a short climb, the view is very good.

Access to the trailhead is off Rt. 28 between the villages of Indian Lake and Blue Mountain Lake. It is on the west side of the road, 2.6 mi. (4.2 km) north of the bridge across the Cedar River. This is about 6.0 mi. (9.7 km) from Blue Mountain Lake village. The well-marked trailhead has excellent parking facilities.

The trail follows yellow DEC trail markers up rolling grades from the road, leveling off after a few minutes. A moderately steep grade then takes you over a small shoulder of a ridge and down again. Red paint blazes are mixed with occasional trail markers for the rest of the route. Climbing becomes generally moderate for the next half hour.

The pleasant trail passes to the left of a large boulder at 0.9 mi. (1.5 km). The path then levels for a short while and leads to a lookout to the east. The bare rock slope is rather steep and is biased down to the left. Immediately after starting out on the rock, the trail cuts to the right, reentering the woods. Walking is much safer there. The trail farther upslope returns to the open, where good views are found.

Trees become more widely spaced as you approach the wooded summit. The trail goes on another 270 ft. (83 m) past the summit to an excellent lookout.

Below to your left front is Sprague Pond. Beyond it, Blue Ridge extends for several miles. In the valley to your right is a beautiful vlei. Looking due west, between the vlei and the pond, thin Stephens Pond is seen high up on the ridge. The Northville–Placid Trail skirts this pond as it winds 132 mi. (214 km) through the Adirondacks. In the far distance, Blue Mountain stands out boldly on the horizon.

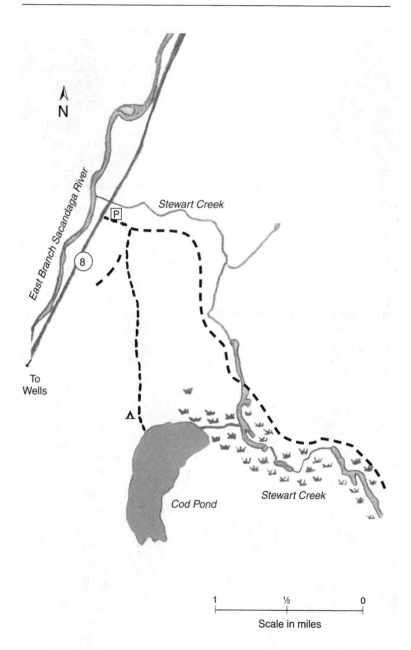

Cod Pond (trail 13)

Eagle Bay and
Blue Mountain Section

The Eagle Bay and Blue Mountain section is in the Lake Region of the Adirondacks. The terrain is relatively flat and is more suited to sustaining the wear and tear of the hiker's boots. Though many trails are heavily used, they retain an amazing freshness and primitive quality.

There is something special about this region. It takes hold of you and won't let go. Alvah Dunning, the hermit, lived in the Blue Mountain Lake area in the middle 1800s. Encroaching summer vacationers forced him on to Raquette Lake and, later, to Eighth Lake. When guideboats became too frequent there, he really became upset. He lit out for the Rocky Mountains for peace and quiet. He was back within a year. These lakes had cast their spell over him and he could not stay away.

The lake country mountains are generally not big. You can take your time climbing them and really observe your surroundings. Yet, since the whole region is so flat, excellent views are gained from the summits of these peaks. Rts. 28 and 30 lead into this region.

15. Rondaxe (Bald) Mountain
Round-trip Time: 1 hr. 30 min.
Round-trip Distance: 2.0 mi. (3.2 km)
Elevation Change: 400 ft. (122 m)
Summit Elevation: 2350 ft. (719 m)
Difficulty: Easy, with only one minor steep spot.
Maps: Old Forge 7.5'; or Old Forge 15'; or Old Forge metric

The hardest thing about this mountain is figuring out what to call it. At first, it was Pond Mountain. For a while it became Foster's Observatory in honor of Nat Foster, the trapper. He said he liked to go there to get away from the Indians. After the Civil War, there was a movement by some summer residents to call it Mont. St. Louis. Now, almost everyone calls it Bald Mountain, except for the state officials. To avoid confusing it with another fire tower mountain having the same name, the Conservation Department opted to call it Rondaxe Mountain. Why Rondaxe? Named after a nearby lake, it is the phonetic corruption of the last two syllables of Adirondacks.

On any account, it's one of the most frequently climbed mountains in the Park. For sheer fun and ease of climbing, it can't be beat. The summit view is superb.

Access to the trailhead is on Rondaxe Road, off Rt. 28 between Eagle Bay and Old Forge. Turning west on Rondaxe Road, drive 0.2 mi. (0.3 km) to where there is a large parking area on the left side of the road.

A large, wooden map of the area and a DEC register mark the trailhead. Follow red markers. The first five minutes of walking take you through a hardwood forest on an essentially level trail.

The only steep climbing begins at this point, leading up bare rocks and over tree roots. This short stretch soon moderates. The first lookout is at 0.3 mi. (0.5 km).

Beyond here the climb continuously provides ever-widening views of the Fulton Chain to the east. The ease of climbing combined with frequent looks at the scenery bring you to the summit before you expect it.

The trail follows a hogback ridge. Its spine tapers until, at the last, you feel you are walking up the vertebrae of some great extinct dinosaur.

The rain shelter and fire tower are seen after about 30 minutes of hiking. Below you to the east, large Fourth Lake meets your gaze. As your eyes swing to the right, Fourth Lake constricts to a narrow channel and becomes Third Lake. Second and First lakes are seen farther to the right. Beyond First Lake is Little Moose Lake. Turning back to the far end of Fourth Lake to the left, Blue Mountain looms above the distant horizon 28 miles away. Over 56 miles distant, Mt. Marcy can be seen on a clear day in line with the extreme left margin of Fourth Lake. Algonquin is to the left.

Closer in, Black Bear Mountain is seen just past the end of Fourth Lake. Seventh Lake is to its right. Wakely Mountain may be seen in the distance, over the broad part of Fourth Lake.

16. Moss Lake Circuit Trail
Round-trip Time: 2 hrs.
Round-trip Distance: 2.5 mi. (4.1 km)
Elevation Change: minimal ups and downs.
Difficulty: Easy.
Maps: Eagle Bay 7.5'; or Big Moose 15'; or Eagle Bay metric

Moss Lake is a quiet body of water, around which are found pleasant hiking and skiing trails. There is little, today, to signify its importance in Native American affairs in New York State. The lake and surrounding land was site of the Moss Lake Camp for girls from the early 1920s until 1973, when it was sold to Nature Conservancy. Immediately resold to New York State, the property became part of the Forest Preserve. With some legal basis, members of the Mohawk Nation impounded the land in 1974 and named it Ganienkeh (Land of Flint), after the ancient name for Mohawk lands. Soon, shots were fired and local citizens were wounded, but Native Americans continued to live off the land until 1977. Mario Cuomo, then New York Secretary of State, became involved in 1976, and soon thereafter a lease-trust arrangement near Altona in Clinton County resulted in a land exchange and peace.

Only a few stone walks and the remains of some building foundations hint of its past, as nature continues to encroach on the shoreline, and dirt

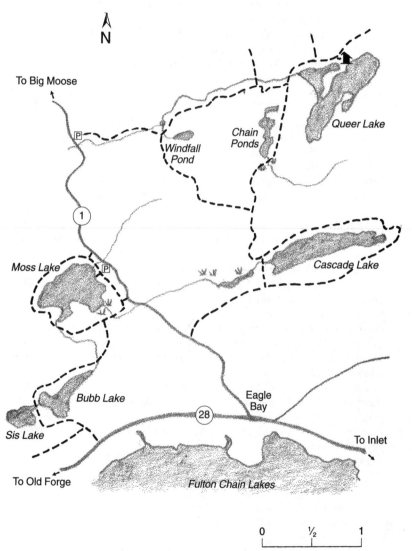

N

To Big Moose

P

Windfall
Pond

Chain
Ponds

Queer Lake

1

Moss Lake

P

Cascade Lake

Bubb Lake

Eagle
Bay

28

Sis Lake

To Inlet

To Old Forge

Fulton Chain Lakes

0   ½   1

Scale in miles

Moss Lake Circuit (trail 16) and
Windfall Pond Walk and Loop Option (trail 17)

lanes have become enchanting woods roads where solitude and beauty reign once again.

Summer trailhead access is found 2.1 mi. (3.4 km) along Big Moose Rd., from Eagle Bay. A parking area, trail register, and photo board are found on the west side of the road. (A winter trailhead access is found at the 1.7-mi. [2.0 km] point on this road.)

The lake and beach is 135 yds. straight ahead. The Circuit Trail around the lake, with its yellow DEC trail markers, intersects the beach path only a short way from the parking area. Turning left, the Circuit Trail heads southeast, sometimes near the water and sometimes further back from a view of the lake. Occasional side paths lead to the location of past building sites on the lakeshore.

At 0.4 mi. (0.6 km), the winter trailhead access road enters at the left from Big Moose Rd. and, after another few minutes of walking, a bridge is reached, which crosses Cascade Lake outlet, the main inlet of Moss Lake.

Another yellow-marked trail enters from the left at 0.7 mi. (1.1 km); this point is also the unidentified junction to Bubb and Sis Lakes. Hikers of the Circuit Trail should take care to continue straight ahead.

(If a longer trip is desired, one can walk south from this junction 0.7 mi. [1.1 km] to the northeast corner of Bubb Lake, 1.6 mi. [2.7 km] to Sis Lake, or 1.8 mi. [2.9 km] to the south end of Bubb Lake. This is a hemlock-surrounded route that offers fairly level skiing in winter.)

The Circuit Trail continues generally west, before swinging to the northwest. Crossing a bridge at 1.2 mi. (1.9 km) when it reaches the Moss Lake outlet, a good view of Moss Lake's south bay is gained. Lovely mixed wood forest occupies your interest along the trail. Before long the trail drops down to the lake edge, which is followed for some time as you now travel northward. At 2.0 mi. (3.2 km), an open fern area is crossed and a number of side trails (one of which has stone steps) to former buildings near the lake's northern shore are seen.

Finally, at 2.4 mi. (3.8 km), the trail turns right, heading south, while the short route straight ahead continues on to the Big Moose Rd. You are soon back to the starting point at 2.5 mi. (4.0 km).

Perhaps its time for lunch at the beach or some paddling on the lake to explore its small island.

17. Windfall Pond Walk and Loop Option

Round-trip Time: 1 hr. and 30 min.
Round-trip Distance: 2.2 mi. (3.6 km)
Elevation Change: 180 ft. (55 m)
Difficulty: Easy.
Maps: Eagle Bay 7.5'; or Big Moose 15'; or Eagle Bay metric

The Windfall Pond Trail makes a nice little afternoon hike. It can be extended to a full day's outing if desired. The trail basically parallels the pond's outlet creek. Sometimes high above, sometimes right alongside, it is a pretty path that takes you along the brookside up to the pond.

Access to the trailhead is the large DEC parking area on the Big Moose Road from Eagle Bay. This parking area is on the northeast side of the road 3.3 mi.(5.3 km) from Eagle Bay and 0.6 mi. (1.0 km) south of Higsby Road.

Starting at the DEC register, follow yellow trail markers along an open level path. At 0.1 mi. the trail turns sharply to the left and crosses the creek on a wooden bridge. Watch for this turn so as to avoid confusion with a footpath leading straight ahead to a well-established campsite.

The trail soon climbs a gentle grade far above the creek before descending gradually back to the water and a second bridge crossing at 0.7 mi.

Turning left across the bridge, the trail parallels the stream. The flow widens to form a vlei in places. At 0.9 mi. (1.5 km) the outlets of Queer Lake and Windfall Pond meet at a swampy area called Beaver Meadow.

Following the brook upward another few minutes brings you to Windfall Pond. This pretty little body of water is inundated with white lilies. The purple spikes of pickerel weed brighten the shorelines.

A full day's outing can be had by going on from the trail junction at Windfall Pond. Following the yellow trail to the left for another 1.6 mi. (2.6 km) will bring you to Queer Lake after joining the red Cascade Lake trail near the lake. After seeing Queer Lake, backtrack on the red trail and follow it past Chain Ponds toward Cascade Lake for 1.4 mi. (2.3 km) to where it meets the blue trail back to Windfall Pond. Turning right, it is another 1.2 mi. (1.9 km) along the blue trail back to Windfall Pond. This would make a total day's walk from the trailhead and return of about 6.5 mi. (10.5 km).

18. Black Bear Mountain
Round-trip Time: 3 hrs.
Round-trip Distance: 4.4 mi. (7.2 km)
Elevation Change: 542 ft. (181 m)
Summit Elevation: 2448 ft. (749 m)
Difficulty: Easy, with one steep section.
Maps: Eagle Bay 7.5'; or Big Moose 15'; or Eagle Bay metric

Black Bear Mountain is an attractive peak. The first part of the trail runs over the old Uncas Road, built by J. Pierpont Morgan. He and the other elite rode over it to his camp on Mohegan Lake in a coach drawn by six plumed horses. The mountain burned over once, leaving it barren on top. Slowly recovering, much of its summit is a fascinating collection of lichen, blueberries, and mountain ash. Views in all directions are excellent.

Access to the trailhead is on Uncas Road, off Rt. 28 in Eagle Bay. Turn north from Rt. 28 at the DEC sign for Browns Tract Ponds Public Campsite.

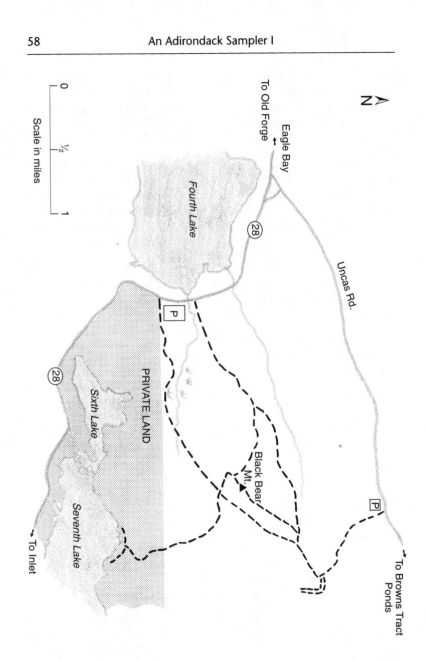

Black Bear Mountain (trail 18)

This road bears left almost immediately and becomes a hard-packed dirt road. The trailhead is 2.9 mi. (4.7 km) down this road on the right side. Here, a sign indicates it is 3.5 mi. (5.7 km) to Eighth Lake Public Campsite. There is parking for several cars.

The trail initially follows the original Uncas Road, which is now a grassy lane. A short way along this route a cable stretches across the trail. Long, very moderate, grades make progress easy. As you near the bottom of one of these grades, at 0.9 mi. (1.4 km), you see a sign on a birch tree. It points to a side trail at the right. The summit is 1.3 mi. (2.1 km) in that direction.

Turning right, you drop down a moderately steep grade. The otherwise excellent trail has grown in some at this point but soon widens again. Crossing a brook at the bottom of the grade, you proceed along an easy trail. You again drop down a grade and cross another creek at 1.1 mi. (1.8 km).

As you climb a short, moderately steep grade at 1.2 mi. (2.0 km), a ski trail sign is passed on the left. Avoid this turn. Continue straight ahead where you will follow yellow nordic ski trail markers for the rest of the way.

Avoid an unmarked trail to the right a few minutes later, just before reaching a marked junction. The trail to the summit follows the expert ski trail straight ahead. The regular nordic ski trail branches right, running for another 3.0 mi. (4.9 km) to Rt. 28.

The next section of trail is much steeper than anything else to this point. As it winds upward through the trees, there is a branch off left to a lookout. You can walk the rim of the mountain for a short distance before returning to the main trail. Beyond the lookout, the path moderates. It breaks the tree line, covering the last 0.2 mi. (0.3 km) on open rock. Rock cairns guide you where the yellow markers aren't posted. In this section be sure you see the next cairn or marker before leaving the one you've just passed.

The summit is spectacular both for its unusual lichen vegetation and its view. The main vista is to the southeast. Seventh Lake stands out, with large Goff Island at its center. Beyond, Fawn Lake Mountain is seen, with Limekiln Lake to its right. Behind you to the north, Cascade Ridge extends toward Raquette Lake. Blue painted arrows take you a short distance westward over the rocks to another good vantage point. From there, Fourth Lake can be seen. Plan on spending a long time on this most interesting summit.

The trail, and especially the summit section, would appear much more suited for snowshoeing than for skiing. In fact, the trip in over the ski trail from Rt. 28 to the summit would make a nice 6 mi. (9.7 km) round trip. This ski trail begins on Rt. 28 0.9 mi. (1.5 km) east of Brown's Tract Pond Road and is marked by a small sign. The route along Uncas Road is a snowmobile trail in the winter and probably isn't plowed from Rt. 28.

19. *Blue Mountain*

Round-trip Time: 3 hrs.
Round-trip Distance: 4.1 mi. (6.6 km)
Elevation Change: 1569 ft. (478 m)
Summit Elevation: 3759 ft. (1146 m)
Difficulty: Moderately difficult; middle section is steep.
Maps: Blue Mountain 7.5'; or Blue Mountain 15';
    or Blue Mountain Lake metric

Called *To-war-loon-da* by the Indians, this mountain is truly a "Hill of Storms." Its great bulk stands above the surrounding territory like a giant sentinel. In the days of Verplanck Colvin, gunpowder flashes were set off at this summit each evening precisely at nine o'clock to help synchronize the work of his survey crews.

Trailhead access is located on the edge of Blue Mountain Lake village just north of the Adirondack Museum. From the junction of Rts. 28 and 30, this is 1.3 mi. (2.1 km) up the hill along Rt. 30. You'll find a large parking area on the east side of the road. Periodic lumbering on the private land at the base of the mountain may require temporary rerouting of the trail.

Trails for Tirrell Pond and Blue Mountain both begin here. An interpretive brochure for Blue Mountain is available at the trailhead. Take the red-marked trail to the right along a nearly level woods road. There is a slight increase in grade just before the route becomes a footpath and enters the woods.

Easy grades alternate with level terrain to provide pleasant walking for the next 15 minutes. You then reach a stream crossing. More challenging climbing is found beyond this point.

The way becomes increasingly rocky until you are climbing over solid sheets of bare rock through the forest. It is unusual and comfortable on the feet. The trail becomes very steep for awhile.

The change is most welcome when the trail levels again at 1.5 mi. (2.4 km). Still on bare rock, the path takes you through a pretty coniferous forest for the last 0.6 mi. (1.0 km) to the summit.

While good views are possible from the ground, the fire tower provides magnificent sightings. To the west Blue Mountain Lake is at the foot of the mountain. To its left are Eagle Lake and then Utowana Lake. Beyond the ridges Raquette Lake can be seen. To the north Minnow Pond, Mud Pond, South Pond, and finally part of Long Lake can be traced. In a northeastward direction, Tirrell Mountain, with its beautiful sandy Tirrell Pond, is below you. Just to the left and beyond is Tongue Mountain. Algonquin is in line with Tongue Mountain, another 25 mi. (40.5 km) in the distance. To the right of Algonquin the gap of Avalanche Pass and then Mt. Colden can be seen. Somewhat farther to the left is Ampersand Mountain, seen between Seward and the much closer Kempshall Mountain on Long Lake.

Blue Mountain Lake from Blue Mountain

Adirondack Museum

20. Cascade Pond

Round-trip Time: 3 hrs.
Round-trip Distance: 5.6 mi. (9.1 km)
Elevation Change: 361 ft. (110 m)
Difficulty: Easy.
Maps: Blue Mountain 7.5'; or Blue Mountain 15';
    or Blue Mountain Lake metric

Enchanting is the term to describe this trail. It is not a place for hurrying. If you would relax in the midst of beauty, this is the place to do it.

Access to the trailhead is off Rt. 30 east of Blue Mountain Lake village. At 0.9 mi. (1.5 km) from the intersection of Rt. 28 and 30, 0.6 mi. (1.0 km) past the St. Lawrence and Hudson Rivers Divide sign, turn right onto Durant Road. If coming from the east, Durant Road is 2.3 mi. (3.7 km) past the Lake Durant Public Campground sign and just past the lake itself. Travel 0.2 mi. (0.3 km) down Durant Road to the trailhead sign on the left side of the road. It is just before you reach a cemetery. Your vehicle may be left here or can be parked a short distance down the trail road. Please do not block the passageway.

From the paved road, follow red DEC trail markers a short distance to where an arrow on a sign points to an abrupt turn to the right. Crossing a small brook, the path follows a level route before ascending a tiny knoll.

The trees are an unusual mix. Large hemlocks overshadow the small balsam firs that are coming in. Before you realize it, you are dropping down a slope to Rock Pond. This extension of Lake Durant is crossed on a 200-ft. (61 m) wooden bridge. The white waterlilies, current-drawn grasses, and purple spiked pickerel weed give you reason to pause. Gazing out on this quiet water, you understand the meaning of "forever wild."

Continuing, you soon surmount a short steep section as you top a little ridge. The trees are now maple and beech. A rather steep but brief descent into the next valley brings you to the second joy of this trip.

For the next twenty minutes, you travel 0.5 mi. (0.8 km) up a delicate valley between two high ridges. The trees are of smaller diameter and are farther apart here. It is like being in a huge amphitheater. Again you feel a distinct urge to walk slowly in order to see everything. It is quite beautiful.

Finally, at the end of the valley, you ascend a moderate slope where the trail becomes essentially level for the remaining 0.9 mi. (1.5 km) to Cascade Pond. You come to a DEC sign 0.5 mi. (0.8 km) from Cascade Pond. Just beyond the sign, bear left. Avoid the unmarked trail to the right.

The trees have now changed to mostly spruce. Cascade Pond is seen at the right a few moments before you reach the lean-to, which sits above the pond. This large beautiful body of water has an active beaver colony.

If a second car is available to the party, a loop ending at the Northville–Placid Trail parking area near the Lake Durant Public Campground is possible. By continuing along the pond edge on the red DEC trail for another

0.9 mi. (1.5 km) you will reach the Northville–Placid Trail. Turning left here, follow blue markers another 2.7 mi. (4.4 km) to the Lake Durant Public Campground. There are excellent swimming facilities there. Blue markers will take you past the swimming area and on to the roadside parking location. This would make a total loop of 6.4 mi. (10.4 km).

Jim Appleyard

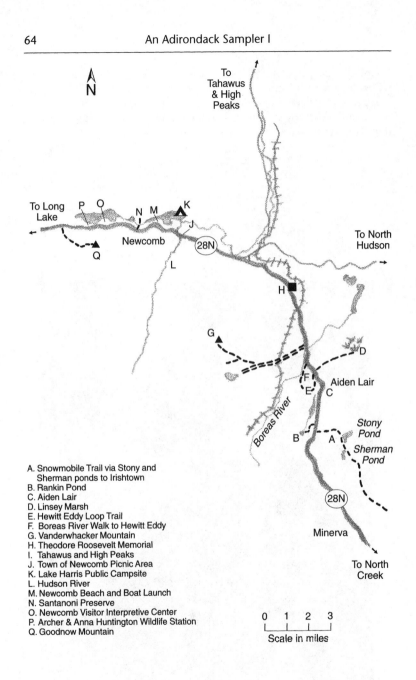

A. Snowmobile Trail via Stony and
    Sherman ponds to Irishtown
B. Rankin Pond
C. Aiden Lair
D. Linsey Marsh
E. Hewitt Eddy Loop Trail
F. Boreas River Walk to Hewitt Eddy
G. Vanderwhacker Mountain
H. Theodore Roosevelt Memorial
I. Tahawus and High Peaks
J. Town of Newcomb Picnic Area
K. Lake Harris Public Campsite
L. Hudson River
M. Newcomb Beach and Boat Launch
N. Santanoni Preserve
O. Newcomb Visitor Interpretive Center
P. Archer & Anna Huntington Wildlife Station
Q. Goodnow Mountain

Rankin Pond (trail 21), Boreas River Walk (trail 22),
Vanderwhacker Mountain (trail 23), and
Goodnow Mountain (trail 25)

Minerva–Newcomb Section

The region between Minerva and Newcomb provides an amazing combination of interesting recreational opportunities. To a large extent it has been ignored as hikers followed the major highway systems into the high peaks. Even those traveling to Tahawus and the complex of trails branching northward to Lake Colden and Mt. Marcy seem not to have been aware of what they were passing by.

Reference to the accompanying map will indicate several of the possibilities for outdoor activities. Harris Lake Public Campground makes a good base for those staying in the area for an extended length of time. Backpackers and cross-country skiers will find Santanoni Preserve very satisfying. The Newcomb Visitor Interpretive Center is a wonderful place to spend a day learning about the Adirondacks and wandering beautiful trails.

There are canoe and boat access sites at both Newcomb and Harris Lake. Mountains with spectacular views of the high peaks are found here. Charming jaunts into flowering marshes and along gurgling brooks make delightful day trips. All things considered, this is a splendid place to enjoy nature.

The sequence of trips provided in this section begins where the Olmstedville Road intersects Rt. 28N at Minerva. It continues along Rt. 28N northwestward to Newcomb and slightly beyond.

21. Rankin Pond

Round-trip Time: 30 min.
Round-trip Distance: 0.8 mi. (1.3 km)
Elevation Change: 100 ft. (32 km)
Difficulty: Easy, with some gradual ascent on the return.
Maps: Dutton Mountain 7.5'; or Newcomb 15';
 or Dutton Mountain metric

A small turnoff with a signpost is found at the trailhead on the west side of Rt. 28N, 4.3 mi. (6.9 km) north of Minerva. There is a small parking area on the opposite side of the road.

The blue-marked trail turns abruptly left almost immediately and winds its way through a hardwood forest. It soon begins a gradual descent over a rocky path and quickly reaches the water's edge.

A small shoreline clearing lends a magnificent view of the pond. The distant shore is cloaked with blueberry bushes. Water plants gracefully reach up through the water to the sky above. It's a quiet place and quite beautiful.

22. Boreas River Walk

Round-trip Time: 1 hr. 30 min.
Round-trip Distance: 2.2 mi. (3.6 km)
Elevation Change: 20 ft. (6 m)
Difficulty: Easy.
Maps: Tahawus 7.5'; or Newcomb 15'; or Newcomb metric

Many years ago there was a state campsite on the Boreas River where it crosses Rt. 28N. Today only a few remaining fireplaces give witness to the past. The river crossing is 8.7 mi. (13.9 km) north from Minerva. Recently a new concrete bridge was built across the river. The approach to the old bridge makes a good parking area. It is adjacent to the old campsite.

The trail begins on the west side of the road, opposite the parking area. It follows red DEC markers along the river bank for the whole distance. The stream's varying sounds are intriguing. First silent, then noisily rushing, it continuously whets your curiosity. Numerous little side trails lead to the river's edge and interesting sights. One notices the fragrance of the conifers and the softness of the earth beneath one's feet.

It's hard to imagine that this little stream once carried thousands of logs downstream each spring as dammed meltwaters were released. Log drivers, mostly French Canadians, leapt nimbly from log to log as they worked to prevent jams.

The trail rambles on with but a single rise above the river. At one point the rushing water draws you to a rocky waterfall. Occasionally a small tributary is crossed.

At the 1.1 mi. (1.8 km) point, the Hewitt Eddy Loop Trail joins the Boreas River Trail at Hewitt Eddy. Do not stray from the river's edge unless you wish to make the loop hike. The Hewitt Eddy Loop Trail runs 0.75 mi. (1.2 km) farther through the woods to Rt. 28N, some 0.6 mi. (1.0 km) south of the Boreas River bridge. If both trails are to be walked, it is suggested that you start at the Hewitt Eddy Loop Trail trailhead.

It was once possible to proceed farther downriver for a different view of Hewitt Eddy, but that section is no longer maintained.

23. Vanderwhacker Mountain

Round-trip Time: 5 hrs.
Round-trip Distance: 5.8 mi. (9.3 km)
Elevation Change: 1650 ft. (495 m)
Summit Elevation: 3385 ft. (1016 m)
Difficulty: Moderate for experienced hikers, possibly challenging
      for novices.
Maps: Tahawus 7.5'; or Newcomb 15'; or Newcomb metric

Named after an early pioneer who lived at the base of the mountain, Vanderwhacker Mountain stands alone. Its summit presents a beautiful vista to the north, where the high peaks rise.

The approach is a gravel road on the west side of Rt. 28N. This is 8.8 mi. (14 km) from Minerva, just across the Boreas River bridge. A small DEC sign and a mailbox mark the turnoff.

This road immediately climbs a steep, loose-gravel slope. Once this hazard is surmounted, the remainder of the 2.6 mi. (4.2 km) drive is better. The driver must, however, use normal caution. Traveling through a beautiful coniferous forest, one feels no desire to rush, anyway. Avoid the left-hand turn at 1.5 mi. (2.4 km) just before reaching Vanderwhacker Brook on a small bridge. There are several open campsites with picnic tables and fireplaces in this area.

The road bears right, crossing a railroad track. One notices the road narrowing and more care is required from this point onward. At 2.6 mi. (4.2 km) a right turn abruptly brings you to a small parking area, a picnic table, and the trailhead. This is the first turnoff since the railroad tracks; it is marked by a very crude sign reading "Vanderwhacker Mountain."

Following red DEC markers, the trail gradually climbs through a hardwood forest. Soon leveling off, it swings right as it skirts a swampy area and crosses two small streams.

More gradual inclines then take you upward for another 20 minutes. Just after crossing a stream at 1.3 mi. (2.1 km), the grade steepens and you can see the fire observer's cabin up the open slope. The snowmobile trail turns left, below the cabin, but the hiking trail passes between the buildings and continues uphill. Situated on a grassy grade, the cabin is a good place to take a rest.

The route leads past the buildings and is much steeper for some distance. Eventually it moderates and finally becomes a path along a narrow ridge. This is a marvelous section of the trail. With the open sky above and the trees sloping off steeply below on each side, it is exhilarating.

Various small herbs and flowers grow here. Occasional ferns add to the scenery. When present, balmy breezes make the setting complete.

Becoming steeper again, the trail ascends one last stretch before emerging at the small sharp peak. It is closed in by trees on three sides, but open views are clear to the north. The fire tower is again open, and the panorama is most rewarding. Algonquin and Avalanche Pass stand out. Mt. Colden, Redfield, Marcy, Haystack, Allen, Gothics, Sawteeth, Nippletop, the Boreas Range, Dix, McComb, and countless minor peaks are evident. Plan on staying on top for awhile.

In winter, the approach road makes an excellent cross-country skiing area through to the fire observer's cabin. It also would be a good climb up the mountain on snowshoes.

The Adirondack High Peaks from Vanderwhacker Mountain

Richard J. Nowicki

ROOSEVELT MEMORIAL TABLET

A stone monument with a metal tablet honoring President Theodore Roosevelt is located on the north side of Rt. 28N, 12.7 mi. (20.3 km) north from Minerva. This is 2.2 mi. (3.5 km) east from Newcomb.

On September 6, 1901, President McKinley was wounded in an assassination attempt in Buffalo, New York. Assured that McKinley was recovering, Vice-President Roosevelt struck out for the Tahawus Club and Mt. Marcy. On Friday, September 13th, his climbing party, having ascended Mt. Marcy, was enjoying lunch at Lake Tear of the Clouds when a messenger burst out of the woods and informed Roosevelt that McKinley had taken a turn for the worse.

This resulted in a hasty withdrawal to the Tahawus Club and an eventual midnight race by horse-drawn carriage to a train standing by at North Creek, ready to speed him off. The monument marks the approximate spot Roosevelt had reached in his dash through the night when, at 2:15 a.m. on September 14, McKinley died and Roosevelt became President.

Roosevelt Memorial Tablet

24. *Newcomb Visitor Interpretive Center*
Map: Newcomb 7.5'; or Newcomb 15'; or Newcomb metric

This center is a marvelous place for both young and old to learn more about the Adirondacks. Workshops, scheduled lectures, and group classes are available year-round. Audio-visual displays in the main building, computer-assistance systems for selecting desired activities throughout the Adirondacks, and picnic tables outside make for a pleasant day.

The Newcomb Center is located off NY 28N, 14 mi. (22.4 km) east of Long Lake village. If approaching from the east, drive west of Newcomb village a short distance until you see the Visitor Interpretive Center sign with the the blue heron silhouette on the north side of NY 28N. This marks the entrance to the center.

Three beautiful trails run along Rich Lake with information posts at regular intervals. Numerous vistas offer seats where the walker can rest, enjoy the scenery, and perhaps think about nature. Some trails are handicapped accessible and canoeing is permitted on the waterways. These trails are:

RICH LAKE TRAIL: 0.6 mi. (1.0 km) loop that is rated easy and takes 45–60 minutes. The user travels on a boardwalk along the lake. Sighting areas allow viewing of Goodnow Mountain and wildlife.

SUCKER BROOK TRAIL: 1.6 mi. (2.6 km), rated moderate and takes 60–90 minutes. You walk through ancient cedar groves and along the outlet of Rich Lake.

PENINSULA BROOK TRAIL: 0.7 mi. (1.1 km), rated challenging and takes 60 minutes. Beautiful cedar and hemlock groves reward the hiker. You also will cross a wetland area on a pontoon bridge.

Vacationers in the area may wish to contact the center to find out about special classes and films of interest for children and adults. VIC offers great rainy day activities for youngsters.

25. *Goodnow Mountain*
Round-trip Time: 3 hrs. 30 min.
Round-trip Distance: 3.8 mi. (6.1 km)
Elevation Change: 1040 ft. (317 m)
Summit Elevation: 2690 ft. (820 m)
Difficulty. Easy for experienced hikers, moderate to easy for novices.
Maps: Newcomb 7.5'; or Newcomb 15'; or Newcomb metric

This trail is found on the Archer and Anna Huntington Forest property of Syracuse University's College of Environmental Science and Forestry. Perhaps no other mountain in the Adirondacks offers such a rich reward for so little effort as does Goodnow Mt. It is truly a gem. This has been especially true since 1993, when the lower trail was rerouted, benches were added for resting and interpretive pamphlets were provided for the hiker.

A climb on this mountain, in conjunction with a visit to the nearby Visitor Interpretive Center, is a very nice way to spend a day with nature. Goodnow Mt.'s new parking area and trailhead is located off NY 28N, 1.5 mi. (2.4 km) west of the Visitor Interpretive Center near Newcomb. It is marked by a large white sign. This point is also 11.4 mi. (18.5 km) east of Long Lake village. You may pick up an interpretive pamphlet and sign the trail register at a kiosk before heading up the mountain. Red trail markers with black arrows guide the way along the trail.

The route enters the forest from the parking area, climbing moderately for about 200 yds. (218 m). It then swings to the right. Small rises and dips are traversed as the route follows a shelf parallel to the highway. Maple, birches and other hardwoods make up the forest growth.

A bridge spans a small brook at 0.5 (0.8 km) and then the trail swings left. Moderate climbing starts at 0.7 mi. (1.1 km). Steady climbing is found before the pathway reaches a ridge crest, joining the old trail at 0.9 mi. (1.5 km) .

Turning sharply left, the forest growth opens up as the old woods road winds its curving course upward. This section is easily traveled and is rather attractive. Massive rocks form cliffs on the right with beds of fern at their feet. A short path leads to the right at 1.5 mi. (2.4 km), where an old covered well stands. The road now curves back to the left. An arrow on a Goodnow Mountain sign directs you to a narrowing path where a second building is passed.

Your route is now along the side of a ridge and is a pleasant journey. Views begin to open up. In a few moments, you drop down into a small col. Avoid a side trail to the left which follows the col downward. Far below in the distance is Rich Lake. Its deep-blue color is in sharp contrast to the emerald green of the forest trees.

A tower sign points straight ahead, and another five minutes along this trail brings you to the fire tower and an old observer cabin at 1.9 mi. (3.1 km). The mountain is fairly open on its rocky top. Absolutely spectacular views are available to the west, north, and east. Climbing the fire tower extends your sighting radius to a full 360 degrees.

All of the High Peaks are visible past the beautiful waters of Rich Lake. To the east, Vanderwhacker's fire tower can be spotted. Far to the west, Long Lake flows northward. As Robert Wickam once said while speaking of another area, "After gazing awhile, the inclination comes to murmur amen."

It would seem that a winter trip up Goodnow Mountain would be tremendously interesting. The trail is wide and easily followed. It is a short trip, but Santanoni Preserve is nearby should additional exercise be desired.

View from Hurricane

Jim Appleyard

Keene–Keene Valley Section

The Keene–Keene Valley section epitomizes the Adirondacks for mountain climbers. It is in this region that many of the "High Peaks," those over 4000 ft. (1223 m), are found. It is here that Orson Schofield ("Old Mountain") Phelps had the feeling of "heaven up-h'istedness" as he gazed from "O'Mercy" (Mt. Marcy).

This results in a curious imbalance, however. While the masses are climbing the giants, the most casual glance at a map will indicate dozens of other peaks that are nearly neglected. If these "little giants" were in other parts of the Adirondacks, they would be scaled far more frequently. It is from these often-forgotten mountains that many of the truly panoramic views of the Adirondack range are found. The hikes described here are representative of the variety of outing opportunities in this region.

Access to this section is by Rts. 73 and 9N, off Exit 30 of the Northway (I-87).

26. Sunrise Trail to Gilligan Mountain

Round-trip Time: 3 hrs.
Round-trip Distance: 2.2 mi. (3.6 km)
Elevation Change: 670 ft. (204 m)
Summit Elevation: 1420 ft. (433 m)
Difficulty: Short, steep slopes alternating with long, gradual sections.
Maps: Rocky Peak Ridge 7.5' and Elizabethtown 7.5';
    or Elizabethtown 15'; or Elizabethtown metric

This mountain is a jewel snuggled in the shadow of much higher peaks. Formerly known as Sunrise Mt., its trail has remarkable variation and vegetation. A series of rock outcrops provide superb views throughout the ascent. It has a few short steep sections, but they are a small percentage of the whole trip.

Trailhead access is from Exit 30 of the Adirondack Northway (I-87). Head northwest on Rt. 73 toward Lake Placid. At 2.4 mi. (3.9 km), bear right at the large jct. Continue northeast on Rt. 9. Pass over a small bridge at Split Rock Falls at 4.7 mi. (7.6 km). This is a good swimming spot to cool off at after the climb. Near a dirt road jct. on the east side of Rt. 9 at 6.0 mi. (9.7 km) is a small, green "Gilligan Mt." sign and a Public Fishing Area parking area. Park here and follow the dirt road across the bridge over the Boquet River. Past the bridge, bear right and continue another 250 ft. (91 m) to the Gilligan Mt. trailed on the left side of the road.

The trail is a flat path which soon crosses a lumber road. It continues on the level through attractive deciduous forest until a moderately steep section is reached at about 0.1 mi. Varying grades and level zones then alternate, passing viewing spots at rock outcrops. Just as one begins to huff and puff, a nice view appears to ease the situation.

The first of several dips in the trail is found at 0.3 mi., with an accompanying short, steep climb out of the low spot. The route changes direction occasionally and there is a sharp drop-off to the left at 0.5 mi. Soon Rt. 9 can be seen in the valley below.

Past lumbering has created open spots where sunlight can reach the forest floor; here swatches of seasonal flowers can often be seen. A beautiful lichen garden graces a lookout spot at 0.6 mi. A series of dips and lookouts, with occasional rock cairns to guide you, takes you ever higher. Volcano-like Hough and the large bulk of McComb and East Dix are now apparent on the west-southwest skyline. The pathway eases in difficulty until a last steep ascent takes you to an open-rock lookout at 1.0 mi.

This is the usual endpoint of the hike, although there is a final trail sign on a tree a short distance ahead. One can continue beyond that point on several herd paths another 0.1 mi. to the actual summit, but trees prevent a view.

All in all, this little mountain, whose trail is maintained by the Schenectady Chapter of ADK, is a wonderful climb of moderate difficulty and short duration, with widely varying views and botanical interest.

27. *The Brothers Trail and Loop Option*
Round-trip Time: 5 hrs.
Round-trip Distance: 5.0 mi. (8.1 m)
Elevation Change: 2198 ft. (672 m)
Summit Elevation: 3721 ft. (1138 m)
Difficulty: Moderately difficult, but steep in one place.
Maps: Keene Valley 7.5' series; or Mount Marcy 15';
    or Keene Valley metric

The following trail description is in two parts. The hiker who wants absolutely beautiful scenery in the context of an afternoon jaunt over bare rock is advised to hike to the summit of the Third Brother. On the other hand, the well-conditioned hiker who wants a full day's trip couldn't choose a nicer way to spend the day than to tramp the loop option.

Access to the trailhead is off Rt. 73. Turn at the large DEC "Trails to the High Peaks" sign in the village of Keene Valley. Drive 1.6 mi. (2.6 km) to the parking area, called the Garden.

Note: Parking at the Garden is limited. There is a town parking fee ($5/day, 2001) collected at the Garden from mid-May through Columbus Day. Overnight parking is also available at the public parking area located on Rt. 73 just south of the village. On weekends in the summer a shuttle bus is

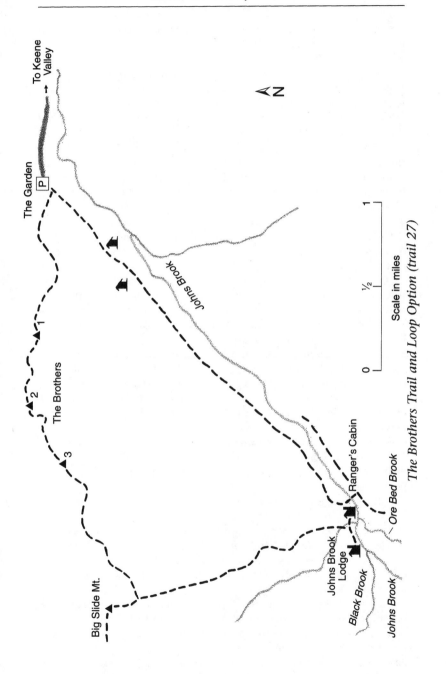

The Garden

To Keene Valley

The Brothers

Big Slide Mt.

Johns Brook

Johns Brook Lodge

Ranger's Cabin

Ore Bed Brook

Black Brook

Johns Brook

N

Scale in miles

0   ½   1

The Brothers Trail and Loop Option (trail 27)

available to transport hikers from the overflow lot at Marcy Field, located just north of Keene Valley on Rt. 73, to the Garden and back ($3 round-trip, 2001).

The trail begins at the right rear corner of the parking area, following red ADK markers up a moderately steep slope. Be careful not to take the yellow Phelps trail, which starts at the left rear of the parking area.

The trail soon levels to a moderate grade and a pleasant walk takes you through the white birches above Juliet Brook. After 20 minutes, the trail turns left and drops down to the stream. Soon after crossing Juliet Brook, the hardest climbing of the trip begins. Becoming a steep grade, the trail swings to the left between two boulders. At rock outlooks, you have excellent views of Hurricane Mountain to the northeast and Giant to the east. Mt. Marcy is in the southeast.

From 1.2 mi. (1.9 km) onward, there is mostly open rock climbing to the flat summit of First Brother. Here, Johns Brook Valley spreads before you. Across the valley the Great Range of Lower and Upper Wolf Jaw, Armstrong, and Gothics are seen.

The trail descends slightly and then continues gradually upward to the summit of Second Brother. A good outlook is found 20 yds. (18 m) off the trail to the right.

The path enters trees and drops through a birch and fern woods. From here it again heads upward toward the summit of the Third Brother. The appearance of balsam fir tells you that higher elevations are being reached. From the Third Brother, which is more closed in than the other summits, the profile of the bare slide of Big Slide Mountain stands out before you. There is no other peak quite like Big Slide in all of these mountains. *The afternoon hiker is advised to go no further.* The return route provides different perspectives of interesting scenery.

The well-conditioned hiker who wishes a longer trip may well continue. The whole loop from The Garden takes approximately seven hours to complete. From this point onward, the trail is harder to navigate and is in poorer condition.

The continuing path drops into a balsam fir and spruce forest. At 2.7 mi. (4.4 km) a natural rock shelter is seen at left. The col is reached 15 minutes later. A gradual climb to the junction with Slide Brook Trail now begins.

The junction is reached at 3.6 mi. (5.8 km). From here, the hiker may turn right for another optional side trip. It is an extremely steep 0.3 mi. (0.5 km) to the summit of Big Slide Mountain. If you have the energy, it is worth the extra time to make the trip.

Turning left down the Slide Brook Trail, descend the slopes through berry bushes to the floor of Johns Brook Valley. Views of the Great Range are frequently seen through the trees across the valley as you follow Slide Brook. A spring is passed soon after beginning this stretch, but it doesn't always have water. Slide Brook appears halfway down the slope and is crossed and recrossed many times.

When the Phelps Trail is reached, a left turn takes you back toward your starting place at the Garden. You may wish to turn right and take the short 10-minute walk to Johns Brook Lodge (JBL). JBL, a wilderness lodge owned and operated by the Adirondack Mountain Club, is unique to the Adirondacks and well worth seeing.

Yellow markers take you along Johns Brook on your return to the Garden. Soon after crossing Slide Brook for the last time, you will see Howard lean-to on the right. Another few minutes down the trail, a trail junction and register are reached at the ranger's cabin. Take the branch to the left and continue following yellow markers up the steep grade.

Rolling terrain with occasionally moderate grades will be traversed for the last 3.0 mi. (4.9 km) of this outing. This attractive, though heavily traveled, section passes through hardwood forests.

Three large boulders are reached 1.4 mi. (2.3 km) from the Garden. One is often used for emergency shelter, as the blackened smoke on the overhang indicates. Deer Brook lean-to is soon reached after a short, steep little climb from the brook. Another 15 minutes of walking brings you to Bear Brook lean-to. From here, a persistent decline in elevation eases the way for the last 0.9 mi. (1.5 km) to the Garden.

28. Hopkins Mountain via Mossy Cascade Brook

Round-trip Time: 4 hrs. 30 min.
Round-trip Distance: 6.3 mi. (10.3 km)
Elevation Change: 2120 ft. (648 m)
Summit Elevation: 3183 ft. (973 m)
Difficulty: Moderate, perhaps challenging for the novice.
Maps: Keene Valley 7.5' and Rocky Peak Ridge 7.5'; or Mount Marcy and Elizabethtown 15'; or Keene Valley metric and Elizabethtown metric

The walk to the waterfalls on Mossy Cascade Brook is charming. The climb along the brook is through hemlock; frequent lookouts and seasonal blueberries add to the pleasure, topped off with an open summit from which 22 major peaks are visible up through the Ausable Lakes and Johns Brook valleys.

The trailhead is off Rt. 73, 0.4 mi. (0.6 km) towards Keene Valley from the Ausable Club entrance sign at St. Huberts. Park at the next St. Huberts side road, 0.1 mi. (0.2 km) from the trailhead. A green and white Adirondack Trail Improvement Society (ATIS) signpost and trail markers on the north side of Rt. 73, where the bank drops from the road, mark the trail.

The trail crosses Crystal Brook and then follows above the East Branch of the Ausable through woods until it nears a home at the left at 0.4 mi. (0.6 km). Swinging right onto a tote road, it immediately turns left to another old road. Finally, the trail bears right at a junction and curves southeast over flat terrain.

The trail leaves the road at 0.5 mi. (0.8 km) and follows the left bank of Mossy Cascade Brook. (Soon a side path left is reached, leading 200 yds. to the base of Mossy Cascade Brook Falls.) The summit trail bears right, passes to the left of a private camp, and then heads up several steep pitches.

The first open lookout is reached at 1.5 mi. (2.4 km). The route then descends into a col before climbing to another broad ledge where more viewing is possible.

The trail moderates before reaching the Ranney Trail junction at 2.3 mi. (3.7 km). (The Ranney Trail heads left 1.8 mi., 2.9 km, to Keene Valley.) The route enters a ravine between Hopkins and Green Mountains. It reaches another junction at 3.0 mi. (4.9 km). Turn left. (The trail right leads 3.0 mi., 4.9 km, to the summit of Giant Mountain.)

The trail climbs very steeply from this junction for a short distance. It then moderates and runs over open rock to the summit. The view up the Ausable Lakes Valley and Johns Brook Valley is magnificent. Enjoy lunch and don't eat all the blueberries.

From the summit, a trail leads northwest 0.7 mi. (1.1 km) to the lookout near the summit of Spread Eagle Mountain.

29. Hurricane Mountain

Round-trip Time: 4 hrs. 30 min.
Round-trip Distance: 5.3 mi. (8.6 km)
Elevation Change: 2000 ft. (611 m)
Summit Elevation: 3694 ft. (1130 m)
Difficulty: A moderately strenuous climb for a fairly long ascent distance.
Maps: Rocky Peak Ridge 7.5'; or Elizabethtown 15';
　　or Elizabethtown metric

The Indian name for Hurricane Mountain is *No-do-ne-yo*, Hill of Wind. Its vast bulk is often buffeted by strong air currents. Alfred Billings Street, the famous lawyer and librarian of 19th-century Adirondack lore, commented on this in his book, *The Indian Pass:* "It put me in mind of the Scripture question, 'What went ye out in the wilderness to see? A reed shaken with the wind?' No, but a crest shaken (nearly) with a whirlwind. Most appropriately named is that peak. The wind fairly poured a torrent over it. I have an indistinct recollection of dim shapes and fluttering garments huddling together for mutual protection from the wolfish blasts, while I clutched the rim of my hat with the clutch of desperation. But the view was superb."

Carry a jacket or sweater with you for comfort at the summit. Pick a good day and enjoy that superb view. It's one of the best in the mountains.

The trailhead is on the north side of Rt. 9N, 3.6 mi. (5.8 km) east from Rt. 73 and 1.6 mi. (2.6 km) past Hurricane Road. This is 6.8 mi. (11.0 km) west from Elizabethtown. It is marked by a small DEC signpost and there is a parking area on the opposite side of the road.

The trail follows red DEC trail markers. It immediately climbs steeply up from the road for about 15 minutes. Leveling off, a footpath now passes through attractive coniferous forest. Soon, significant numbers of bog bridges takes you over a wet area.

Having traveled easily a little over a mile (1.8 km), you will now find climbing more challenging. Heading up a ridge, long moderate grades with periodic respites take you upward. Take care to follow markers straight up the mountain when you reach the small blowdown section. Do not extend the false trail to the left, as some earlier hikers have done. Another wet section is crossed on corduroy as you approach the 2.0 mi. (3.2 km) point.

Once past this section, climbing picks up again. The change from coniferous to birch trees at this elevation is a reminder of past forest fires. Just before joining the ADK North Trail from the Mountain House, the trail again steepens sharply and is quite rocky.

Turning right at this junction, the trail levels and the last 265 yds. (243 m) to the summit pass through wind-stunted spruces to the bare rock. Paint blazes now take you generally to the left and guide you to the base of the fire tower. A full-circle panorama makes it unnecessary to climb the tower.

To the north you can see the Jay Range. The Green Mountains of Vermont spread out beyond Lake Champlain in the northeast. Directly southward is Knob Lock, with the ridge of Green Mountain beyond it. Giant and Rocky Peak Ridge are still further off. Dix, Nippletop, the Great Range, and finally Mt. Marcy are seen as your gaze swings southwestward. Mt. Colden and the MacIntyre Range are seen next. These are followed by Cascade and Porter. Pitchoff is due west, with distant Ampersand just to its left. Whiteface Mountain is northwest. Lesser peaks, too numerous to list, are found in all directions.

30. Balanced Rocks on Pitchoff Mountain
Round-trip time: 2 hrs. 30 mins.
Round-trip Distance: 3.1 mi. (5.0 km)
Elevation Change: 882 ft. (270 m)
Summit Elevation: 3022 ft. (924 m)
Difficulty: Half is easy, half is on a very steep eroded trail.
Maps: Keene Valley 7.5'; or Mt. Marcy 15'; or Keene Valley metric

The Balanced Rocks on Pitchoff Mountain provide both a climb and viewing location that are quite unusual. The hiker should be prepared for some steep climbing and an eroded trail. The small ridge that holds the Balanced Rocks has an appearance more of the Swiss Alps than of the Adirondacks. Expect an interesting outing.

Access to the trailhead is off Rt. 73 at the north end of Upper Cascade Lake. This is 4.5 mi. (7.3 km) east of Heart Lake Road. Park in the area provided at the Cascade Mountain trailhead and climb the Pitchoff Mountain trail directly across the road.

Red DEC trail markers take you up a moderately steep grade for about five minutes. The route then levels for the next 0.5 mi. (0.8 km). You first find an attractive open maple stand and then a spruce-birch wood.

About 20 minutes after starting your climb, you ascend a steep pitch to a small lookout at the right. Cascade Mountain stands out. Another longer pitch brings you to a better lookout, where both Cascade Lakes are clearly seen in their glory below. The sharp cut in Cascade Mountain between the two lakes was the original trail up that peak. It leads to the cascade of water from which the mountain gets its name.

Moving along the ridge side, you soon drop down to a flattened depression, which is quickly crossed. Steep climbing then begins. After ascending one such section, the trail swings left on the level for a short distance. A second steep eroded section follows, until you reach the bare rock face of a near vertical slope at 1.1 mi. (1.8 km).

The old trail to the right is considered dangerous. The safer route follows red markers to the left. Here, you spend the next 15 minutes sidling around the bald wall of the mountain. You soon descend slightly, and then begin a moderate, but steady, climb to the upper end of the rock massif. A junction is reached at 1.4 mi. (2.3 km).

Turn right for Balanced Rocks. On a welcome level stretch the whole character of your surroundings makes a dramatic metamorphosis. Low conifers thin out as you move toward the end of the ridge. A barren, windswept aura of desolation develops. Void of vegetation, the two great balanced rocks perch at the extreme point of the ridge, seemingly ready to fall into the great abyss below. Giant eroded joint patterns in the rock floor give the whole scene an appearance of being ready to collapse at any moment, but they have been this way for millennia. Beyond Balanced Rocks, the ridge's vast rounded edge juts toward Lake Placid in the distance.

To the left stands Cascade Mountain, overshadowing all else. Algonquin is seen behind her, along with Big Slide, Colden, and Marcy. Hurricane is in the east. Behind you is the first summit of Pitchoff.

This is a good place to have lunch. You may want to walk a short way south of Balanced Rocks to a ledge offering a splendid view of the Cascade Lakes.

The trip can be extended on a pretty trail by continuing from the junction up to the first peak of Pitchoff Mountain. The trail narrows considerably and is quite easy. The round trip to the summit and back to the junction will add another 45 minutes and 1.1 mi. (1.8 km) to your outing. The summit elevation is 3600 ft. (1101 m).

STAGECOACH ROCK

A little-known monument between Lake Placid and Keene commemorates the passing of the day of the stagecoach in the Adirondacks. Some 4.6 mi. (7.5 km) east of Heart Lake Road is a boulder at a pulloff on the north side of Rt. 73. (This is just downhill from the trailhead to Cascade Mountain, across the road from Upper Cascade Lake.) Carved into the large rock are a stagecoach, team, and driver.

From 1855 to 1890, the stagecoach was the primary means of public conveyance in the mountains. The main stations were Elizabethtown, Keeseville, Ausable Forks, and North Creek. From these locations, routes spread out through the North Country to interior towns and resort hotels.

For fifteen years, Fred Cook drove six horses over the treacherous Spruce Hill Road from Elizabethtown. "Fitch" O'Brien hauled passengers up through the much-feared Wilmington Notch. Ike Roblee headed up to Blue Mountain and Long Lake from North Creek. Dozens of other skilled drivers safely carried their charges through the woods until the "iron horse" and "horseless carriage" put them to pasture.

Ralph Geiser

Stagecoach Rock

One day in the 1930s, Donald Rogers, a district engineer working on highways, was at work when a large boulder fell to the roadside off Pitchoff Mountain. Thinking it too nice to simply push aside, he had the forethought to see a use for it. Eventually Louis Brown of Carnes Granite Co., Inc., made a sketch and Wilfred Carnes sandblasted the outline of the stagecoach and team onto the boulder. It is a fitting tribute from the highway department to a mode of transportation of another era.

31. Noonmark Mountain from Round Pond
Round-trip Time: 5 hrs.
Round-trip Distance: 6.7 mi. (10.9 km)
Elevation Change: 1991 ft. (609 m)
Summit Elevation: 3556 ft. (1087 m)
Difficulty: A steady climb of fair effort.
Maps: Dix Mountain 7.5' and Underwood 7.5'; or Mount Marcy 15' and
    Elizabethtown 15'; or Mount Marcy metric and Witherbee metric

Noonmark gets its name because the sun stands directly over it at noon as viewed from Keene Valley. This middle-sized peak presents a panorama of great beauty. From its bare-rock pinnacle can be seen most of the major peaks.

Access to the trailhead is the Round Pond Trail off Rt. 73. This is 1.1 mi. (1.8 km) southeast of Chapel Pond and 3.0 mi. (4.9 km) northwest of the intersection of Rts. 9 and 73. It is on the southwest side of the road. A large parking area is just north of the trailhead.

The 0.6 mi. (1.0 km) hike into Round Pond is a moderate but steady climb over a well-used route. During the ten-minute walk, you follow red DEC trail markers to the top of a grade and then drop down toward the pond. Before reaching the water's edge, the trail turns right. It begins a level swing around the north shore of the water. This pretty section has an unusual amount of both white birch and cedars.

Pulling away from the pond, you begin a steady ascent. For the next half hour the trail changes from a moderate to a moderately steep slope, following a stream up a col on the south edge of Round Mountain. At 1.6 mi. (2.6 km) the trail levels, then descends slightly and finally levels again. A junction is reached at 2.3 mi. (3.8 km).

The blue-marked Dix Trail from St. Huberts crosses your route here. Orange ATIS (Adirondack Trail Improvement Society) trail markers take you straight ahead, up the Felix Adler Trail toward the summit of Noonmark. Moderately steep to steep grades are found on this section of trail. Some interesting rock cuts are passed.

About a half hour later, the first lookout is reached as bare rock and spruces appear. Dix Mountain and Nippletop are seen to the south. As elevation is gained, several more lookouts are passed. Soon Round Top, Giant, and Rocky Peak mountains are seen to the right, to the northeast. The trees decrease in both number and size. One last rise takes you to the bald summit, where the whole eastern High Peak region is before you. The emerald carpet of conifers spreads out toward the Great Range. Gothics is spectacular. Mt. Marcy is to the left of Gothics. Beyond the Great Range, Johns Brook Valley and The Brothers are seen. The Dix Range is to the south. Hunter's Pass cuts sharply between Dix Mountain and Nippletop. Spend a long time on this summit.

32. The Crow Mountains

Round-trip Time: 3 hrs.
Round-trip Distance: 2.7 mi. (4.4 km)
Elevation Change: 1220 ft. (373 m)
Summit Elevation: 2800 ft. (856 m)
Difficulty: Steep but short.
Maps: Keene 7.5' and Jay Mountain 7.5'; or Elizabethtown 15' and
  Ausable Forks 15'; or Lake Placid and Lewis metric

The joy of these two small peaks is the immense amount of open-rock climbing found here. Excellent views are available for the time expended. Take a good book and spend a long afternoon on top of the world.

Access to the trailhead is off East Hill Road from the village of Keene. The ADK trailhead is on the north side of the road, 2.1 mi. (3.4 km) from Keene. Note the mileage carefully, since the trailhead is identified only by a red ADK trail marker. Parking is found a little farther down the road from the trailhead. The Mountain House is 0.23 mi. (0.3 km) beyond the trail.

The trail winds through an open hardwood stand to a pine woods. Red ADK markers then take you on a 15-minute, steady climb to the beginning of the rocks. You pass a large boulder, a huge U-shaped rock, and an immense oak tree.

Turning right at a vertical rock face, you start angling up the side of Little Crow Mountain. The trail is now almost entirely over rock. Outlooks soon appear as you very rapidly gain elevation. Cairns and paint blazes mark much of the way. Passing below the west summit of Little Crow, you next reach the flat, easy summit.

An unmarked cairn junction is found here. It is easy to miss. Cairns lead left to a very large rock pile at 0.9 mi. (1.5 km), indicating the true summit. Summit elevation is 2540 ft. (778 m); the ascent has been 960 ft. (294 m). The cairns then lead back to the trail over to Big Crow Mountain. Had you followed the cairns to the right of the junction instead of going to the Little Crow summit, they would have led you to this location.

Big Crow Mountain stands before you. You must carefully follow the cairns and markers as you drop down to the wooded col between the two peaks.

Steep climbing now takes you up the meandering route to the bare summit of Big Crow Mountain. It is a beautiful spot. Directly back over

Little Crow, huge Cascade Mountain looms in the distance. To the left, down the valley, is Giant. Farther left, in the southeast, is Hurricane Mountain, easily located because of its fire tower. Much closer, to the north, is the Nunda-ga-o Ridge (Soda Range).

The return trip offers many options. The reverse of the ascent is suggested if only one vehicle is available to the party. If you have a second vehicle, a most enjoyable descent can be made to the south, ending at Big Crow Clearing. The second vehicle could be left there by turning left onto O'Toole Road just past the Mountain House. The clearing is the state's trailhead for this mountain and is 1.2 mi. (1.9 km) up O'Toole Road. You can make this loop even if you don't have a second vehicle, but it means walking on a dirt road for over a mile.

Lake Placid, Saranac Lake, and Paul Smiths Section

The Lake Placid and Saranac Lake section is distinct because it is the transition zone of the two Adirondack land divisions. To the south and east of Lake Placid lie the High Peaks of the Mountain Belt. Beyond the Saranacs to the west is the Lake Region.

It was this beautiful setting that attracted such greats as Ralph Waldo Emerson, Louis Agassiz, and William James Stillman in the mid-1800s. What fascinating conversations must have echoed across the waters at their "philosophers' camp" on Follensby Pond and later at Ampersand Pond. It took the Civil War to prevent this group from continuing its annual summer gathering.

The country is just as inviting today as it was in yesteryear. Many combine canoeing with hiking here.

33. Ampersand Mountain
Round-trip Time: 4 hrs. 30 min.
Round-trip Distance: 5.4 mi. (8.7 km)
Elevation Change: 1775 ft. (543 m)
Summit Elevation: 3352 ft. (1025 m)
Difficulty: First half is easy, second half very steep and rugged.
Maps: Ampersand 7.5'; or Santanoni 15'; or Ampersand Lake metric

Standing on Ampersand Mountain, you can gaze into the bold face of the Seward Range and then to the more distant High Peaks. Turning around, you can look below to the Saranacs and the lake country. Such a contrast in beauty is not available to this degree anywhere else in the Adirondacks. This bald summit has long been a favorite, though you must work to earn your reward.

The trailhead is located on Rt. 3, 12 mi. (19.4 km) east of Tupper Lake and 8 mi. (13 km) south of Saranac Lake village. A large parking area is on the north side of the road, with the trailhead signpost on the south side. Dropping over the back edge of the parking area is a 0.5 mi. (0.8 km) trail leading to a day use area at Middle Saranac Lake. A crescent-shaped beach of "amber sand," from which this region is thought to have gained its name, makes an after-climb swim hard to resist.

The trail begins at a small downslope. Past it, a broad path takes you along a level route through a woods having an almost park-like quality. For 20 minutes, the beauty of well-spaced hemlocks keeps your interest. A few gurgling brooks are crossed before a section of corduroy indicates that changing terrain is ahead.

With the crossing of a shorter, second section of corduroy, moderate climbing begins. At 1.6 mi. (2.2 km), avoid the old trail that goes straight ahead across Dutton Brook at this point.

The new trail swings to the right side of the clearing and follows the creek for a way. The last mile (1.6 km) to the summit is very rugged. Over 1300 vertical ft. (398 m) must be scaled. Very fine stone work steps make it much easier in many places.

Finally, at 2.4 mi. (3.9 km), a col provides a level respite. An extremely large rock overhang is passed under. The trail circles the summit and then a short section of moderately steep grade brings you to the bare rock. Yellow painted markers lead you up the massive rock to the peak.

To your left, in the west, the Saranacs spread out before you. Middle Saranac is smallest and has several islands. Upper Saranac is behind it. Lower Saranac is to its right toward the north. Northeast is Oseetah Lake, with Scarface Mountain at its right. Haystack and McKenzie are beyond Scarface. Whiteface Mountain is still farther off to the northeast. Below you to the southeast is Ampersand Pond. Beyond the pond stands Seward Range and, to its left, Mt. Seymour. Imagine, if you will, a little firecracker of a man snowshoeing up Ouluska Pass between those two mountains. He is headed for Coreys on his annual visit to civilization at Christmas time. Such a man actually existed. His name was Noah John Rondeau and he did this every year for over a quarter of a century.

Closer in, to the left of Ampersand Pond, is Van Dorrien Mountain. Just over its shoulder is Algonquin, thrusting 5114 ft. (1564 m) skyward in the distance. To the south is Kempshall Mountain on Long Lake.

Yellow paint markers take you on a short distance to a slightly lower part of the summit. The foundation supports of the old fire tower can still be found here. Nearby, a bronze plate is attached to the rock. It commemorates Walter Channing Rice, "the hermit of Ampersand," who manned the tower for many, many years.

This mountain is often climbed on snowshoes in the winter, though considerable skill is needed for the last mile.

34. Baker Mountain
Round-trip Time: 2 hrs.
Round-trip Distance: 1.8 mi. (2.9 km)
Elevation Change: 884 ft. (270 m)
Summit Elevation: 2452 ft. (750 m)
Difficulty: Short, but steep; tough little climb.
Maps: McKenzie Mountain 7.5'; or Saranac Lake 15'; Saranac Lake metric

This mountain almost was not included in this guide because of its relatively short length. But what it lacks in distance, it makes up in steepness. The view is excellent.

Access to the trailhead is off NY 86 in Saranac Lake Village. When entering the village from Lake Placid, turn right at the traffic island by the NBT branch bank onto McKenzie Rd. Drive over the railroad tracks and turn left onto Pine St. Cross the railroad tracks again and proceed to East Pine St. Turn right onto East Pine St., cross the wooden overpass, and continue to the north end of Moody Pond. A small DEC sign marks the trailhead. There is room here for parking several vehicles along the road.

Follow the unmarked trail up a gradual grade. Bear right and then eventually left at trail forks along the way. All ascending routes eventually merge just below the summit, but all the trails are not equally easy to travel. The general rule is that when there is a choice of routes to follow, take the one that shows the most use.

Once through this short section, which only covers about 0.1 mi. (0.2 km), the way to the summit is clear. It is up. Moderately steep to steep grades take you along your way for a few minutes. Then a welcome level stretch lets you catch your breath. You are ready for the very steep part, which appears at 0.6 mi. (1.0 km).

The trail is wide and not dangerous, but take your time. It is a rather long section of steady climbing. As the trail becomes more rocky, the first red ADK trail markers are seen. Follow them carefully.

A series of lookouts give excellent views of the high peaks to the southeast. Ampersand Mountain is seen to the south, just beyond large Oseetah Lake. The summit provides a good view eastward. Haystack Mountain is seen across McKenzie Pond. The long hulk of McKenzie Mountain is close behind Haystack Mountain. A short path leads north of the summit to a cliff of considerable height. From it you can see St. Regis Mountain, the large bulk of Debar Mountain, and a few other of the outlying peaks to the north. In all, this amazing little peak looks out to 28 major mountains.

35. Scarface Mountain
Round Trip Time: 4 to 5 hrs.
Round Trip Distance: 6.8 mi. (11.0 km)
Elevation Change: 1480 ft. (451 m)
Summit Elevation: 3088 ft. (941 m)
Difficulty: Generally moderate with a few steep spots.
Map: McKenzie Mountain 7.5'; or Saranac Lake 15';
     or Saranac Lake metric

Anyone driving east on NY 86 from Saranac Lake village can see why this mountain has its name. The bold scar of bare rock is particularly noticeable in winter when the snow covered rock contrasts starkly with the green of the trees.

The lower part of the mountain trail takes you through open forest and along rippling brooks. The upper part is more rugged, but short enough to be enjoyable. Just take your time and stop to enjoy your surroundings for a few moments if you find yourself becoming a bit tired.

Access to the trailhead is off of NY 86 in Ray Brook, opposite the DEC Region 5 Headquarters. Turn south onto Ray Brook Rd. and drive 0.1 mi. (0.2 km), to where a trailhead sign and small parking area are found on the left side of the road.

An attractive trail leads through a pine forest before crossing an abandoned railroad bed. The rolling-terrain route brings you to the marshy shore of Ray Brook at 0.5 mi. (0.8 km). The slab lumber walkway and large wooden bridge across the waterway is an ideal spot for photography, as well as a pleasant place for a rest break on the return trip.

Wooden steps lead up a steep bank from the bridge and the pathway levels briefly. It soon begins a gradual ascent, however, arriving at a clearing at 0.7 mi. (1.1 km), where a large boulder is the center of attraction.

When the federal prison was built and used as the Olympic Village at the 1980 Games, the original trailhead up Scarface Mt. was closed. Now, as you continue along the trail, another junction is found at 1.5 mi. (2.4 km), where the original woods road trail up the mountain is reached. (Be careful to note the correct trail for the return trip.)

Turning left, a slight descent occurs and then at 1.7 mi. (2.7 km) the hiking trail turns sharply left again from the woods road. For a while, the pathway is nearly level. After another half mile, a brook is crossed and followed up the mountain for a ways.

Climbing becomes more continuous as a moderately steep ascent begins. Finally the route follows a contour along a broad rock front and then climbs a steep pitch to an open rock ledge at 3.1 mi. (5.0 km). Good views of the surrounding countryside are available here and many hikers may choose to go no further. By bushwhacking a short way to the right, even better vistas are found.

Beyond this point, climbing is much easier, following a narrow path to the ridge line, proceeding easily upward through coniferous woods. Another opening is reached at 3.4 mi. (5.4 km). Here there is a 180-degree viewing zone, from which one can scramble about to see distant Ampersand Mt., the Sawtooth Range, the Sewards, and all manner of bodies of water. Haystack, McKenzie, and Whiteface Mts. are to the north. The only problem is that tree growth is closing off this view more and more each year.

The true summit cannot be reached by trail, requiring a bushwhack to the viewless high point. Viewing is undoubtedly better in the winter. However, the snowshoe ascent requires considerable skill for the steep ascent to the first clearing and might well be hazardous without full crampons when icy conditions exist.

36. *Haystack Mountain*

Round-trip Time: 5 hrs.
Round-trip Distance: 6.6 mi. (10.7 km)
Elevation Change: 1302 ft. (397 m)
Summit Elevation: 2874 ft. (876 m)
Difficulty: A moderately strenuous hike, with short steep sections near end.
Maps: McKenzie Mountain 7.5'; or Saranac Lake 15';
or Saranac Lake metric

It seems there are as many Haystack Mountains in the Adirondacks as there are Mud Lakes. This one is in Ray Brook, near Saranac Lake. The peak is overshadowed by huge McKenzie Mountain but offers a very fine view for a lot less effort. In fact, the whole trip is about as nice a day hike as anyone could ask for. The view from the top is excellent.

The old trailhead behind DEC Region 5 Headquarters in Ray Brook was moved in 1984. Today, the trailhead is at a road pulloff on Rt. 86, 1.6 mi. (2.6 km) east of the DEC Headquarters building and 1.4 mi. (2.3 km) west of the junction with Old Military Road. The trailhead has a DEC sign and blue DEC trail markers.

The trail quickly crosses a small knoll and a minor wet area. Swinging left, it climbs gradually over two crests before dropping to a small stream at 0.5 mi. (0.8 km).

Across the creek, the route gradually gains elevation along the base of some low ledges to a point where another slight descent begins at 1.1 mi. (1.8 km). A small clearing at 1.5 mi. (2.4 km) offers viewing to the southwest. From there, the terrain changes as the trail tumbles down a winding route, staying mostly to a narrow ridgeline. Then, at 1.8 mi. (2.9 km), the trail merges with the original trail, which comes in from the left.

The old woods road takes you up a grade beside Little Ray Brook to a junction at 2.4 mi. (3.9 km). The Haystack Mountain trail bears left, continuing on the level. (Avoid the McKenzie Mountain trail, which climbs to the right.)

The water-supply dam of the old State Sanatorium is soon passed, and a half hour of tiered ascents begins. Moderately steep to steep slopes alternate with level stretches, preventing tiring. The forest you are passing through is mature maple-beech hardwood.

At 3.0 mi. (4.9 km) rather steep climbing commences; before long, you reach a rocky outlook. A rocky pathway with occasional paint blazes takes you up to the wooded summit. A large, grassy meadow provides an open vista to the east and south.

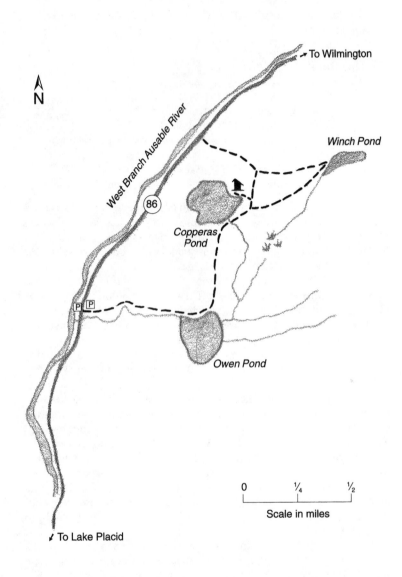

Owen and Copperas Ponds Walk (trail 37)

Walking downslope a short way, one can see Whiteface Mountain to the left, in the northeast. Big Burn Mountain is directly before you. To the southeast, the outline of Algonquin appears to be the largest mountain on the horizon. Mt. Marcy is to her left, looking smaller because it is farther away. Most of the High Peaks can be seen.

Closer in, Scarface Mountain is to the right front, with what was the 1980 Olympic Village at its right. It is now a prison. Farther south is Ampersand Mountain, distinctly separate from the more distant Seward Range at its left. On a clear day this has to be one of the most enjoyable views in the mountains.

A short walk northward through the spruces provides a lookout across the narrow valley to huge McKenzie Mountain. Both Haystack and McKenzie mountains make good winter snowshoeing outings. Haystack is by far the shorter and easier of the two trips and makes a nice six hour climb. McKenzie climbers will probably ascend via the Jackrabbit Trail from Whiteface Inn, starting early and expecting challenges common to a High Peaks bushwhack over the steep winter trail.

37. Owen and Copperas Ponds Walk

Round-trip Time: 2 hrs.
Round-trip Distance: 2.6 mi. (4.1 km)
Elevation Change: 174 ft. (53 m)
Difficulty: Generally easy with a few steep grades.
Maps: Lake Placid 7.5'; or Lake Placid 15'; or Lake Placid metric

A walk at Owen and Copperas ponds can be a two-hour interlude or a whole afternoon of relaxation in the midst of natural beauty. The route described here can be extended by a side trip to Winch Pond. If two vehicles are available, a loop route is possible by leaving the second car at the Copperas Pond trailhead, 1.0 mi. (1.6 km) north from where the Owen Pond trailhead is located on Rt. 86.

Access to the Owen Pond trailhead is on the east side of Rt. 86, approximately 5.0 mi. (8.1 km) northeast of the intersection of Rts. 86 and 73 at Lake Placid. This is about 2.0 mi. (3.2 km) beyond the junction with Riverside Drive, which comes across from the Olympic Ski Jump on Rt. 73. There is parking for a few cars at the trailhead and also parking space on the opposite side of the road.

Blue trail markers guide you along a rolling woodland trail beside Owen Pond Brook. A small grade leads to a hemlock grove, as you travel high above the waterway. Owen Pond is reached at 0.6 mi. (0.9 km). Take the time to go to one of the side paths leading to its shoreline. One of the Sentinel mountains stands out across the water at the far shore.

Moving away from the pond, the pathway soon climbs northward to the top of a hill possessing alternating steep and easy grades. From the crest, one looks down to the right at Copperas Pond. Follow the rocky trail downward to the clearing near the shore at 1.3 mi. (2.1 km), which once held a lean-to. An attractive picture emerges as one gazes across the pond. Great cliffs rise straight upward, with the crest of Whiteface Mountain soaring still higher beyond them as a backdrop. It is truly spectacular.

This short walk changes continuously as the seasons cast their special magic. Early spring flowers spatter the open woods floor. Young buds soon burst into leaves, drawing a veil over the forest. Shadows play their tricks and spiders weave their webs in the warming days of summer. Radiant leaves form a patchwork quilt, with conifers adding just the right amount of green, as autumn suddenly dashes in. Finally, the white snow of winter clears the easel until nature's artist begins afresh in the new year.

For a longer outing, there are many options. Refer to the map on page 90. The hiker may continue on level trail around the east shoreline of the lake 0.1 mi. (0.2 km) to a fork in the trail, where the side trail right leads another 0.5 mi. (0.8 km) to Winch Pond. (The connecting trail is quite attractive, but Winch Pond is not.)

A more interesting option is to bear left at this fork and continue along the lakeshore another 0.3 mi. (0.5 km) to the lean-to on the north shore. Along the way are several rock crops just waiting for someone to lunch on and a deep pool for swimming. If a loop route is desired, the trail to the right at the junction you pass on the way to the lean-to leads steeply up and then down 0.5 mi. (0.8 km) to the second trailhead at Rt. 86.

38. Wanika Falls

Round-trip Time: 7 hrs.
Round-trip Distance: 13.4 mi. (21.8 km)
Elevation Change: 582 ft. (178 m)
Difficulty: A very long trip over easy terrain.
Maps: McKenzie Mountain 7.5' and Street Mountain 7.5';
   or Saranac Lake 15' and Santanoni 15' ; or Saranac Lake metric
   and Ampersand Lake metric

The Wanika Falls hike is a beautiful walk over the north end of the Northville–Placid Trail. The trip is longer than it used to be because of the rerouting of this section of trail in 1977. It is a long day's hike. The trail and falls are worth the effort, however. Endurance and time are factors for consideration. The actual terrain covered is not at all difficult.

Access to the trailhead is off the Averyville Road, south of Lake Placid. Averyville Road intersects Rt. 73 in the village of Lake Placid. If approaching Lake Placid from Saranac Lake on Rt. 86, you may take the Old Military Road to the Northville–Placid Trail (N–P) at the Averyville Road intersection. Old Military Road can also be reached from Rt. 73 near the Lake Placid Horse Show grounds. From the N–P sign at the Old Military Road intersection, drive 1.2 mi. (1.9 km) south on Averyville Road to the Chubb River bridge. A N–P sign indicates the trailhead and a small parking area at this point. A much larger and better parking area is found 900 ft. (275 m) farther down the road at the right.

The trail passes a DEC register and follows blue trail markers along a tote road beside Chubb River for 475 ft. (145 m). Here, it branches left and becomes a foot path. Elevation is gradually gained. The route crosses several tributaries and low divides as it progresses generally southward in a sweeping arc. The undulating course passes through a hardwood forest on a good trail for the next 1.2 mi. (2.0 km).

The next 1.1 mi. (1.7 km) has several soggy spots that must be crossed. They are somewhat dispersed and are of no consequence because of several wooden walkways.

Once past this wet section, you re-enter the hardwoods. The next 3.6 mi. (5.8 km) to Chubb River passes through some of the nicest forest in the Adirondacks. About half an hour after beginning this section, you cross a bridge and begin a long, gradual climb on an old tote road. A gurgling brook is below you to the right. As you reach the top of the grade, the trail branches left, away from the tote road. Soon after, a rather large vlei comes into view on the right. Finally, about three hours after you began this trip, you descend a small grade and connect up with the old N–P Trail cutoff at Chubb River.

A bridge takes you over a high rocky section of the Chubb River. At the far end of the bridge, the original N–P Trail enters from the right. Turning left from the bridge, the route takes you upstream beside the river. For 0.7 mi.(1.1 km) you steadily gain elevation until the water is far below you. The trail levels and you soon reach the trail junction for Wanika Falls. Were you to continue straight ahead for another 124.5 mi. (201.7 km), you would arrive at Northville on the Great Sacandaga Lake, having passed through one of the most remote parts of the Adirondacks.

Turn left and proceed about 500 ft. (153 m) up the steep trail towards Wanika Falls. Some falls are seen here, but the really spectacular falls are found about 0.1 mi. (0.16 km) further upstream. Here, in a series of drops, water cascades several hundred feet to a pool. It is not only beautiful but beckons you to a refreshing swim before lunch.

39. Mt. Jo

Round-trip Time: 1 hr. and 45 min.
Round-trip Distance: 2.3 mi. (3.7 km)
Elevation Change: 710 ft. (217 m)
Summit Elevation: 2876 ft. (880 m)
Difficulty: An easy mountain because of its short distance,
   but steep in places.
Maps: North Elba 7.5'; or Mt. Marcy 15'; or Keene Valley metric

Mt. Jo is a special mountain. In 1877, Henry Van Hoevenberg and his fiancée Josephine Scofield climbed Mt. Marcy to choose, from all they surveyed, the place for their future home. A tiny heart-shaped lake, far to the north, was selected. The mountain near it was soon named Mt. Jo, after Josephine. Then tragedy struck. Josephine died within a year. She was never to see her home completed. But Van Hoevenberg carried on and completed the well-known Adirondack Lodge, which was later destroyed by the great forest fire of 1903. Some years later the Lake Placid Club acquired the property, rebuilding the inn. Melvil Dewey, a driving force behind the reconstruction and a proponent of phonetic spelling, provided his own inimitable mark of peculiar spelling. Today the complex is known as Adirondak Loj and is owned and operated by the Adirondack Mountain Club. Tender memories of a time forever lost linger on this tiny mountain top.

Mt. Jo is on the Adirondak Loj property at Heart Lake. It is reached via Adirondak Loj Road by turning off Rt. 73 at the DEC "Trail to the High Peaks" sign. This is 4.0 mi. (6.5 km) southeast of the village of Lake Placid. At 4.8 mi. (7.8 km) down Adirondak Loj Road, turn left into the public parking area.

From the entrance of the parking area, walk a short distance eastward back down Adirondak Loj Road to the Indian Pass Trail on the left. Follow this trail a short distance, turning right when a T-junction is reached. Cross a small bridge. The Mt. Jo trail begins on the right, immediately beyond the bridge.

The trail is well-marked with blue paint blazes and ADK markers. Leaving the Indian Pass trail, the route immediately turns left and climbs to the junction of the Long and Short summit trails. For a loop trip, ascend via the Long Trail and descend on the Short Trail.

The Long Trail bears left and gradually circles the base of the mountain, with little change of elevation. At 0.6 mi. (1.0 km), a sharp pitch begins your real climbing. At 1.0 mi. (1.6 km), the Short Trail rejoins the Long Trail. From here, the remainder of the trip is easy, with a little rock climbing just before reaching the summit.

Splendid views are found from Mt. Jo. Heart Lake is seen below. Looking southward, the MacIntyre Range of Wright Peak, Algonquin, Boundary, Iroquois, and Marshall opens up. Slightly to the left, over Mt. Colden, Mt. Marcy can be seen. Farther left, over Phelps, the Great Range comes into view. Whiteface Mountain can be seen in the northwest. All in all, this is a very fine observation point for such a short climb.

The return route is the reverse of the ascent until the junction with the Short Trail is reached. The Short Trail branches left. It is quite steep but has some rather unusual rock formations along the way. It does require a bit of agile footwork in places, since some of the trail is heavily eroded, but a number of outlooks make the paint-marked trail interesting.

View east from Mt. Jo

Richard J. Nowicki

40. Paul Smiths Visitor Interpretive Center

Map: St. Regis 7.5'; or St. Regis 15'; or St. Regis Mountain metric

Paul Smiths Visitor Interpretive Center (VIC) offers the outdoor enthusiast opportunities for hiking and paddling in the summer. Skiing and snowshoeing trails are kept open in the winter. The accent is on *interpretation,* thereby providing the visitor with an educational event as well as exercise. Some trails have wheelchair access.

In addition to its guided tours, special events, and scheduled classes, the famed Native Species Butterfly House is found here. Many kinds of native butterfly species and the food species they eat are found in this 30-ft. by 50-ft. screened structure. Volunteer guides help the visitor learn about the life cycles, feeding habits and adaptations of the butterflies.

The Paul Smiths VIC is reached via Rt. 30, 12 mi. (19.2 km) north of Saranac Lake village. It is 0.9 mi. (1.5 km) north of the junction with Rt. 192 at Paul Smiths. Trails are linked to permit many options for time and distance. The following summer trails are found at Paul Smiths VIC:

BARNUM BROOK: 0.6 mi. (1.0 km), rated easy, 45 minutes. Cross four bridges along Heron Brook to Heron Marsh as you pass through an 80-year-old forest.

HERON MARSH TRAIL: 0.8 mi. (1.3 km), rated moderate, 45–60 minutes. Two boardwalks to the edge of the marsh, an elevated platform, and two leantos are along this route.

FOREST ECOLOGY TRAIL: 1.2 mi. (1.9 km), rated easy, 60 minutes. Nine hundred feet (274 m) of boardwalk take you through a scenic bog.

SHINGLE MILL FALLS TRAIL: 0.6 mi, rated easy, 30 minutes. Begins at south end of Heron Marsh Trail, leads you through a scenic marsh, and includes 300 ft. (91 m) of pontoon bridge and a scenic waterfall.

SILVICULTURE TRAIL: 1.0 mi (1.6 km), rated moderate, 45 minutes. Interprets methods and practices used by foresters to manage forest land.

Among the several winter trails is the intermediate-ability 4.5-mi. (7.2 km) Esker Trail and five shorter trails.

41. St. Regis Mountain

Round-trip Time: 3 hrs. 30 min.
Round-trip Distance: 6.8 mi. (10.9 km)
Elevation Change: 1266 ft. (386 m)
Summit Elevation: 2865 ft. (876 m)
Difficulty: Generally moderate, but rather steep for last part.
Maps: St. Regis 7.5'; or St. Regis 15'; or St. Regis Mountain metric

This trail makes a relatively short, steep climb to the summit of an isolated northern Adirondack peak with magnificent views in nearly all directions. A closed fire tower dominates the top. Because it is a non-conforming structure in the St. Regis Canoe Area, it is likely to be removed at any time.

Paul Smiths Visitor Interpretive Center

Overlook on Barnum Brook Trail

A new parking area was built in summer 1999, and the first two-thirds of the trail was rebuilt by a professional ADK trail crew working under DEC auspices. It's an interesting reroute which avoids muddy sections and roller-coaster undulations along the boundary of Camp Topridge.

Access to the trailhead is from the main entrance to Paul Smith's College at the intersection of Rts. 30 and 86. Drive north about 200 yds. and then turn left (west) on Keese Mills Road. Proceed 2.6 mi. to an ample DEC parking lot on the left, just beyond a gravel road leading left to Camp Topridge, the former estate of Marjorie Merriweather Post. Park in the designated parking lot, and not along the private Topridge road.

Leaving the parking lot, walk south down the Topridge road, which immediately crosses the St. Regis River on a narrow metal bridge. At 0.1 mi. take the DEC red-marked trail on the right. Sign the trail register, a few yards into the woods. The trail begins an ascent through mature second growth, with brief level sections at 0.2 and 0.4 mi. At 0.6 mi., note the large maple on the left. Switch-back sharply left at 0.75 mi. and reach a height of land at 1.0 mi. in an impressive stand of large hemlocks. The trail now begins a gradual descent, reaches a low point at 1.5 mi. and resumes a gradual ascent. At 1.8 mi., a metal pipe and cairn on the left mark the boundary between the Franklin County towns of Brighton and Santa Clara. The intersection with the old trail is reached at 2.2 mi. and the trail immediately crosses a perennial brook on a sturdy wooden bridge. Some 35 yds. beyond the bridge, a side trail to the left leads 35 yds. to an open grassy campsite, the former site of a DEC fire tower observer's cabin.

The main trail soon begins to rise more steeply. Impressive water bars, stepping stones, and rock cribs were constructed by Paul Smith's forestry students. At 3.2 mi., the trail passes enormous boulders. At 3.3 mi., a path to the right leads 20 yds. to open bedrock and views westward. The mostly bare summit, dominated by an abandoned fire tower, is gained at 3.4 mi. The bareness of the summit and the presence of white birch attest to earlier clearing by the surveyors under Verplanck Colvin. A few stunted spruce and fir are, as usual, present on the top, along with mountain ash.

The High Peaks, along with McKenzie Mountain and the Seward Range, can be seen to the south. Directly below is a stunning expanse of lakes and ponds within the St. Regis Canoe Area. Eastward, one can see the pointed top of Whiteface with Esther to its left. Slightly to the northeast the isolated peaks of DeBar and Loon Lake Mountains stand out clearly.

This is a fine summit for snowshoeing, but the steepness of terrain in the last mile will discourage all but the most skillful backcountry skiers.

Cranberry Lake, Wanakena, and West Section

The Cranberry Lake, Wanakena, and West section is a relatively isolated area. The old ways still linger here. The people have a pride and friendliness that clearly tell you how much they enjoy this country.

Frederic Remington understood this when he summered at Witch's Bay on Cranberry Lake. The feelings of many others are expressed near the mouth of Sucker Brook on this same lake; there, chiseled into a rock, are words in commemoration of a world-champion, fly-casting champion of yesteryear: "In memory of Reuben Wood, a genial gentleman and great fisherman who was fond of these solitudes." Many today are still drawn to these solitudes.

The river people along the St. Lawrence have passed Sunday Rock for years on their way to the "South Woods." It took the automobile, however, to open the way into this region from other directions. Even the rivers flow northward, away from the larger cities of the state. Now, campers from Syracuse, Rochester, and Watertown frequent the area.

For flatland hiking in an exceptional setting, this is a marvelous section of the Adirondacks. The hiker who also likes to paddle a canoe will find no finer place to combine the two pleasures.

Access to this section is by Rts. 3, 56, and 58. Towns are far apart and traffic is light. Be sure your vehicle is in proper running condition.

SUNDAY ROCK

Four-tenths of a mile (0.6 km) north of the Raquette River bridge in the town of South Colton is a dull, grey boulder. It used to sit along the dusty road traveled by vacationers in their wagons as they headed for the "South Woods" from the Canton area. Natives have long known it as Sunday Rock.

As boulders go, it is unremarkable—rather modest in size, though a bit more regular in shape than most. Its significance is not in substance, but in what it represents.

For some reason, this rock always caught the eye of the tired traveler on his way to a place of revitalization. It was said there was no Sunday beyond this rock. Once past this point, one entered a special world of timelessness where one was freed of the restrictions of more formal society.

When the automobile came along, the narrow road had to be widened. Sunday Rock was in the way. A hue and cry arose throughout the North Country. The Sunday Rock Association was formed to save it. First the *Watertown Daily Times* and later the *Brooklyn Eagle* took up the banner.

Public opinion eventually prevailed. The rock was carefully removed from its position and today sits in its little park with dignity and respect.

The whole thing was a sentimental gesture, but typical of those who love the Adirondacks. They know Sunday Rock represents the spirit that draws them to these woods. Though the physical beauty of this land is immense, it is really the sense of unencumbered freedom in the midst of this beauty that is unique here. The ageless boulder symbolizes their determination that the essence of the Adirondacks shall always survive.

42. Cat Mountain

Round-trip Time: 5 hrs.
Round-trip Distance: 10.2 mi. (16.3 km)
Elevation Change: 766 ft. (234 m)
Summit Elevation: 2261 ft. (691 m)
Difficulty: Easy, but a fairly long trip.
Map: Newton Falls 7.5', Five Ponds 7.5', and Wolf Mountain 7.5'

This trail is part of an immense hiking system into one of the finest wilderness areas of the Adirondacks. Extended trips of over a week are possible in this region.

Access to the trailhead is from the village of Wanakena. Wanakena is 1.0 mi. (1.6 km) off Rt. 3. As you proceed to Wanakena, bear right at any road forks you come to. After you cross the Oswegatchie River on a metal bridge, travel 0.5 mi. (0.8 km) until you reach a small DEC sign indicating Janacks Landing. There is parking just past the gated fire road.

Follow the trail 2.0 mi. (3.2 km) to its end. The almost-level, grassy lane passes through the remnants of the July 15, 1995, microburst storm that changed this area significantly. The route is the old bed of the railroad that Rich Lumber Company ran to Dead Creek flow, where a steam-powered jack lifted logs from the lake to railroad cars for transport. After about 25 minutes of walking, you pass a pretty little vlei on the right. Five minutes later, you catch your first glimpse of Dead Creek Flow on the left. The trail then parallels the flow until the latter's terminus. Janacks Landing can be seen across the water.

The trail continues 0.9 mi. (1.4 km) to another trail junction. On the way, Dead Creek and a second brook are crossed on wide plank bridges designed to accommodate skiers. From the junction, Janacks Landing is 0.2 mi. (0.3 km) to the left. This makes a good swimming spot on the return trip.

Bearing right, you are led by red markers on a flat trail for some 15 minutes. Then you very gradually gain elevation as you pass through a draw. Approaching the end of the draw, the trail becomes a moderately steep grade for a short distance.

Just beyond the height of land, you again come to a trail junction. The Plains Trail goes straight down the slope ahead. Follow the yellow-marked trail, which bears left along the ridge.

Moving on, you soon hear the sound of rushing water. Before long, you reach the cascading waters of Glasby Pond Outlet. The trail follows the

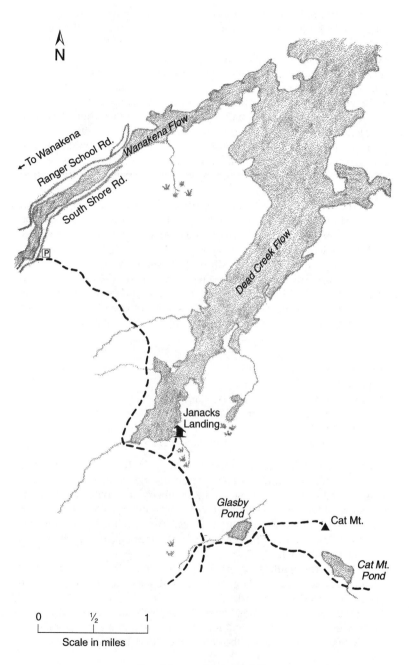

Cat Mountain (trail 42)

outlet a short half mile (0.8 km) to Glasby Pond. A pretty fern meadow is passed through just before you reach the pond. At the pond's edge you cross the outlet. Glasby Pond is a jewel. Its dark water is surrounded by bushes, giving it a primitive look.

The trail soon bears right and for some distance is above the water level, providing a splendid view of the pond and the mountain beyond.

Leaving the pond, the trail begins to climb gradually until a trail junction is reached. The yellow trail to the right leads to Cowhorn Junction. Bear left and follow red markers to the summit of Cat Mountain.

The summit is only 0.6 mi. (0.8 km) ahead. The trail is moderate and levels frequently. Eventually you run straight into a very high massive bluff. The only real climbing occurs here as you climb a very steep 100 vertical feet up a narrow rock path.

At the top the trail swings right, passes a couple lookouts, and soon reaches the summit. Only the foundation of the fire tower remains, but you have a splendid view from the open rock. As you move around the rock bluff to the left, charming vistas appear to the east, where the high peaks are seen in the far distance. Cat Mt. Pond is seen below.

As your eyes sweep the vast forest region, it is hard to believe that all this was desolation in 1908, when sparks from locomotives started fires that devastated the region. The recuperative power of nature is great, but let's hope that man has not forgotten this terrible lesson from our past.

43. *Brandy Brook Flow*
> Round Trip Time: 4.5–5 hrs.
> Round Trip Distance: 6.0 mi. (9.6 km)
> Elevation Change: 125 ft. (38 m)
> Difficulty: Easy.
> Map: Cranberry Lake 7.5'; or Cranberry Lake 15'

The July 15, 1995, microburst storm that struck the Adirondacks devastated the Five Ponds Wilderness Area on the west side of Cranberry Lake. Miraculously, it did very little damage to the Cranberry Lake Wild Forest on the east shore of the lake. The Brandy Brook Flow trail travels over long, gentle grades through attractive deciduous forest. This is not a challenging trip, but it is perfect for one of those days when a leisurely walk, perhaps with binoculars, is desired.

Access to the trailhead is off the south side of Rt. 3, 2.7 mi. east of Cranberry Lake village. Its large DEC signpost, adequate parking area, and exhibit board are easily found.

A brief, easy upgrade guided by red snowmobile markers takes the hiker to the wide open route you will follow all the way to Brandy Brook Flow. At one time this was the roadbed for a Grass River Railroad spur track, on

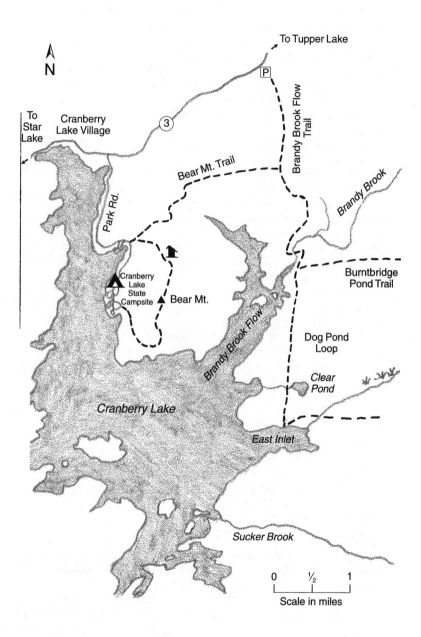

Brandy Brook Flow (trail 43) and Bear Mountain (trail 44)

which lumber was hauled from the region for the Emporium Lumber Company. Now it is a grassy lane cruising over long, gentle grades through a tall forest that makes it hard to believe that lumbering once took place here.

Heading south, the trail soon levels, but descends gently again before reaching a junction at 1.4 mi. (2.2 km). There is a trail register here and a sign that indicates a route up Black Bear Mt. to the west. (The summit is 3.5 mi. [5.6 km] from this point and makes a nice side trip, though occasional beaver flooding may be encountered. A fine view of Cranberry Lake rewards the climber.)

Continuing along the Brandy Brook Flow path, an open meadow is soon passed. Then, at 2.3 mi. (3.7 km) the route makes a sharp turn right and sidles around a wetland that eventually drains into Brandy Brook. This brook is crossed on a low bridge at 2.8 mi. (4.5 km).

Again turning abruptly right, the trail soon passes a footpath on the right leading to a designated campsite along Brandy Brook. At 3.0 mi. (4.8 km), a major junction is reached. The trail to the left (east) runs another 3.6 mi. (5.8 km) to the Burntbridge Pond lean-to. Straight ahead is the Dog Pond Loop Trail, which runs to East Inlet before circling past many ponds to the intersection with Burntbridge Pond trail for a total of 10.0 mi. (16.0 km). A walk along either trail for a short distance is a nice extension to the trip, if more exercise is desired. However, a right (west) turn at this junction on an unmarked path leads a short distance to the shores of Brandy Brook Flow. This is just below the inlet of Brandy Brook and is the farthest up the flow most canoeists paddle. Here you find a grassy launch point for boats and a fine place to have a lunch. From this clearing, you can do some birding, a little fishing, and a lot of soaking up the sun rays.

This is an excellent cross-country ski trail all the way to Burntbridge Pond.

44. Bear Mountain

Round-trip Time: 2 hrs.
Round-trip Distance: 3.6 mi. (5.8 km)
Elevation Change: 742 ft. (227 m)
Summit Elevation: 2242 ft. (686 m)
Difficulty: Easy, with a few steep places.
Map: Cranberry Lake 7.5'; or Cranberry Lake 15'

Bear Mountain is on the north shore of Cranberry Lake and offers a pretty view of the lake. Short enough so that swimming and picnicking can be combined with the climb, it makes a nice little outing.

Access to the trailhead is off Rt. 3 at the Cranberry Lake Public Campground and Picnic Area. This is just east of the village of Cranberry Lake.

Turning at the large sign, drive 1.2 mi. (1.9 km) until you come to the toll booth. There is a small day-use charge. Proceed past the picnic and beach area until at 0.5 mi. (0.8 km) you reach the DEC sign for Bear Mountain. There is a large parking area at the left.

The trail leaves the right rear of the parking area where there is a trail register. Follow red DEC markers. The almost level trail passes through a predominantly beech forest. Quite rocky at first, it becomes more comfortable as elevation is gained.

Two small brooks are crossed. At 0.6 mi. (1.0 km) the grade becomes moderately steep and climbs steadily for a few moments. A short distance from where the trail briefly levels again a lean-to is passed on the left.

After crossing a small brook on a log bridge, the trail again becomes moderate to moderately steep. Soon it swings up to the left and steepens considerably. This is the only really steep part of the trail. You soon reach the top of the mountain ridge and proceed along the flat summit for about 10 minutes.

Here the forest is more open and the trees are somewhat smaller. You actually are slowly losing some elevation. Passing between two immense boulders, you enter an interesting boulder field. Strewn about like so many checkers, the many boulders in this location were dropped by the last glaciers about 10,000 years ago.

The easy walking continues, until at 1.5 mi. (2.4 km) you reach the lookout. From this point you look directly down on Joe Indian Island in Cranberry Lake. To the left is Buck Island. Beyond it at Barber's Point is the Cranberry Lake Biological Station. Run by the forestry school of Syracuse University, it provides remarkable training for future foresters. Just to the right of Joe Indian Island, Dead Creek Flow and the Wanakena Channel begin.

In 1908, fire swept this mountain top. Still earlier, a hunter who was stung by hornets got even by burning their nest and half of the mountain. He was smart enough to keep that a secret for many years.

A loop can be made by continuing along the ridge. It is a very nice trail for 0.9 mi. (1.5 km), but it does mean 1.0 mi. (1.6 km) of walking the paved road back through the park to your starting point after you leave the forest.

Still following the red DEC markers, the trail follows the ridge for a few minutes. Then it descends rather steeply for about five minutes. Moderating, the trail continues through a nice hardwood forest. A very large rock outcrop is passed on the right, at 2.4 mi. (3.4 km). Finally the lake is seen ahead through the trees. After crossing a small tributary of the lake on a rustic bridge, you reach the paved road.

Turn right and follow this road to the first junction. Turn right again and stay on this road until you reach the parking area where you left your vehicle. It will take about 20 minutes of walking to cover this distance.

This isn't the top of the mountain, is it?

Turn right and follow this road to the first junction. Turn right again and stay on this road until you reach the parking area where you left your vehicle. It will take about 20 minutes of walking to cover this distance.

45. *Arab Mountain*

Round-trip Time: 1 hr. 30 min.
Round-trip Distance: 2.1 mi. (3.4 km)
Elevation Change: 760 ft. (232 m)
Summit Elevation: 2545 ft. (778 m)
Difficulty: Easy, with varying grades.
Maps: Piercefield 7.5'; or Tupper Lake 15'; or Piercefield metric

Geographically, this mountain sits at the bottom of an enormous flattened "bowl." Though not great in elevation, it is higher than its immediate surroundings. There are excellent views in all directions from its summit.

Access to the trailhead is off Rt. 3. Between the hamlets of Gale and Piercefield, turn south at the sign for Conifer. At 1.7 mi. (2.8 km) there is a left turn. A large sign points the way to Eagle Crag Lake. The trailhead is 0.9 mi. (1.5 km) farther. A railroad track is crossed 0.3 mi. (0.5 km) before the small DEC sign indicating the trailhead. It is on the left side of the road. Parking is available for several cars on the opposite side of the road.

Red DEC markers lead through a beech-maple forest. A well-designed new trail has replaced the older one. The two criss-cross each other frequently; follow the red markers. The trail rises slowly, leveling off frequently. At 0.4 mi. (0.6 km) a sign indicates a spring to the left. Yellow painted tree blazes lead down the slope some distance to the spring.

Soon after, the trail becomes moderately steep, turning left at a large boulder. Reaching the ridge line at 0.6 mi. (1.0 km), the now nearly level path leads through maple and red-spruce growth. It is quite pleasant after the climbing you've just completed. Two rock outcrops are passed. The trail swings to the right around the second of these. One last rise brings you to the fire observer's cabin and the fire tower. The true summit is slightly farther on, beyond a small col, but the described trail terminates at the tower.

The summit is relatively flat. It is a floral bouquet bordered by berry bushes. To the west is Tupper Lake. Beyond the lake are the high peaks. There is a 360-degree panorama. Mt. Arab Lake and Eagle Crag Lake are below to the southeast. To the north are Mt. Matumbla and St. Regis Mountain. The rim of the horizon is full of mountain ridges.

The grades found on this trail are ideal for snowshoeing. The reward for a sunny winter's tramp to this summit would be great for such a short climb. The fire tower has been reopened for public use through the efforts of interested citizens.

Note: A conservation easement across sections of private land permits access to Arab Mountain except in autumn during big-game rifle season.

Richard J. Nowicki

North–Northeast Section

The North–Northeast section has a somewhat different character from the rest of the Adirondacks. Lake Champlain dominates. The French influence is felt in its people and in the names of such places as the Ausable and Boquet rivers. The heyday of this region was founded on the steamboat, the railroad, and the stagecoach.

Ausable Forks was a primary point of embarkation for stages heading into the high peaks. At one time, the Franklin House in Franklin Falls counted well over a thousand guests each season. This was the gateway to the mountains until the automobile changed travel patterns of vacationers. Now both the stagecoach and the Franklin House have disappeared from the region.

The North–Northeast section has quietly withdrawn from the spotlight, but it still retains its own charm. It is an interesting place historically for the hiker who realizes that a knowledge of the past greatly enhances appreciation of the present. Access to this section is via I-87 (Adirondack Northway) and Rts. 30, 72, 3 and 9.

46. Poke-O-Moonshine Mountain
Round-trip Time: 2 hrs. 30 min.
Round-trip Distance: 2.4 mi. (3.9 km)
Elevation Change: 1280 ft. (391 m)
Summit Elevation: 2180 ft. (667 m)
Difficulty: A short hike, with some steep sections.
Maps: Clintonville 7.5'; or Ausable Forks 15'; or Ausable Forks metric

The historian Beauchamp believed the unusual name Poke-O-Moonshine was derived from the Algonquin words *Pohquis* (it is broken) and *Moosie* (smooth). *Pohquis-Moosie* described the sheer cliffs found on this mountain. Others feel the name simply refers to the haunting glens and supposed spirits of this peak. Whatever the facts, this climb rewards the hiker with outstanding views of Lake Champlain to the east and the high peaks to the southwest. In season, a profusion of ferns borders the hiking trail near the summit.

The trail begins at the south end of the Poke-O-Moonshine State Campsite along Rt. 9, about 12 mi. (19.4 km) north of Elizabethtown and 7 mi. (11.3 km) south from Keeseville. If driving north on I-87, exit at Exit 32 and drive west to Rt. 9. Take Rt. 9 north 9 mi. (15 km) to the campground. If driving south on I-87, exit at Exit 33. Drive a short distance to Rt. 9 and then proceed southward about 3 mi. (3.9 km) to the campground.

The red-marked DEC trail begins at the south end of the campground. A small day-use fee will be levied for parking.

The route soon steepens, and a very high rock formation is reached. Passing it to the left, you come to outlooks after a few more minutes. The last outlook has a bench-shaped boulder that appears to have been put there especially for hikers to rest on. The difficulty in climbing varies considerably over the next half mile (0.8 km). The glen containing the remains of the fire observer's cabin is quite picturesque and provides welcome respite. A lean-to is found on a side trail to the left of the cabin, some 65 yds. (60 m) away. A tote road beyond the lean-to has many blueberries. This is a good place to rest before the final burst to the summit.

The hiking trail bears right from the old cabin foundation, continuing with red trail markers toward the summit. The trail now circles the summit, gradually reaching the fire tower. Many bare ledges are passed along the way. The bare rock summit and its fire tower offer a striking panorama. To the east a sweeping view of Lake Champlain, some 8 mi. (13 km) away, stands out. The Green Mountains of Vermont form a backdrop. Mansfield and Camel's Hump are clearly seen. To the south is Deerfield Mountain, with the Jays behind it. To its left is Hurricane Mountain. Distant Gothics is on Hurricane's right shoulder. To the left of Hurricane Mountain is Giant. Right of Deerfield Mountain is the Sentinel Range, 20 miles away. Whiteface Mountain is almost due west. Lyon Mountain is due north, beyond Baldface, which is farther down the ridge. On a clear day, Mt. Royal, 90 miles off in Montreal, can be seen. The hiker who has the time can spend it well by hiking along the crest of this mountain.

Colvin surveyed from this mountain in the 1870s. The careful searcher may locate a copper bolt indicating this was Station 26 of the survey.

47. Lyon Mountain
Round-trip Time: 3 hrs. 30 min.
Round-trip Distance: 5.0 mi. (8.1 km)
Elevation Change: 1790 ft. (547 m)
Summit Elevation: 3830 ft. (1171 m)
Difficulty: Steep for much of the climb, a rigorous High Peak-type trail.
Map: Moffitsville 7.5'; or Lyon Mt. 15'

Charles Merril was only eighteen in the spring of 1881 when his father sent him up Lyon Mountain. The Rev. Thomas Cook of Troy was suffering from asthma, and it was felt the high elevation might help him; young Merril was his guide. Dozens of mountains could be seen in all directions. On June 20, 1881, a roaring hail and snow storm took them by surprise and they didn't come down for two weeks. It was an exciting adventure, and Merril never forgot it. He went on to become a well-known Adirondack guide.

Access to the trailhead is off Chazy Lake Road on the southwest shore of the lake. This can be reached from Rt. 3, starting at the Chazy Lake Road sign for Lyon Mountain Village at Pickett's Corners. After passing a cross-roads, turn left at the T-intersection 0.6 mi. (1.0 km) from Rt. 3. This is County Rt. 29. Continue along this route and turn right at a crossroads after another 1.9 mi. (3.1 km). You then proceed, still on Rt. 29, for another 5.7 mi. (9.2 km) to a gravel road at the left. This once was the entry road to the former Lowenberg Ski Area. If you are approaching on Rt. 374 from Dannemora, this gravel road would be 1.8 mi. (2.9 km) south from where you pick up Rt. 8.

Proceed along this wide gravel road 0.9 mi. (1.4 km) until you reach an open area where you may park. There is no evidence of the former lodge, as trees continue to encroach upon the open area.

The trail begins at the south end of this open area and follows a gradually ascending hardscrabble road south-southwest. Snowmobile trail markers may occasionally be seen, but you will be high up on the mountain before sparsely placed hiking trail markers are found. Side trails have grown in over the years, but the main route is not difficult to follow (1998).

The route steepens significantly and the road eventually becomes a trail. The remains of a former fire tower observer's cabin is seen. This may be a good place to rest before tackling the next section of trail. The way steepens considerably for the next three-quarters of a mile (1.2 km). It is rocky and you must watch your footing.

From this point, the path almost levels. It takes you through a nice spruce stand. Ten minutes later the tower is before you. The rocky summit has good views. On a clear day you can see the glittering spires of Notre Dame Cathedral in Montreal. Mt. Marcy and the High Peaks are to the south. Northeast of you, Chazy Lake stretches forth. Upper and Lower Chateaugay Lakes are west. By careful observation, it is possible to trace the flow of the Saranac River almost all the way to Lake Champlain.

48. Silver Lake Mountain
Round-trip Time: 2 hr.
Round-trip Distance: 1.8 mi. (2.9 km)
Elevation Change: 900 ft. (274 m)
Summit Elevation: 2374 ft. (724 km)
Difficult: Generally moderate, with some short steep sections.
Map: Redford 7.5'; or Lyon Mt. 15'

This little peak was closed to the public a few years ago, but the trail is now open again for climbers. Once again the surprisingly good views from vantage points on the mountain are available to the hiker for relatively little effort.

Access to the trailhead is off the northwest side of County Highway 1, between Hawkeye and Black Brook. This is 0.8 mi. (1.3 km) southeast of

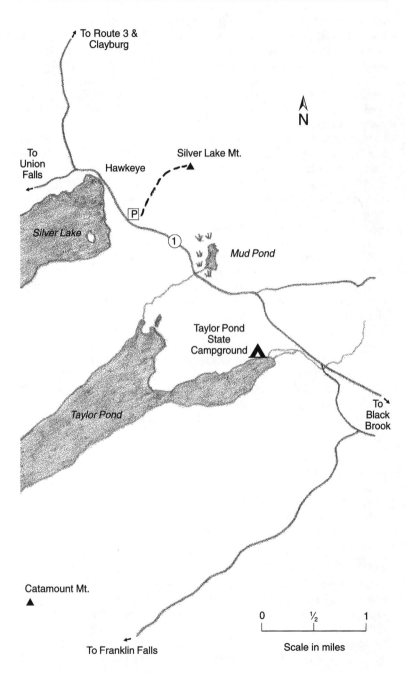

Silver Lake Mountain (trail 48)

Silver Lake at a point where power and telephone lines cross the road. There is a DEC sign at the entrance to a parking area.

The trail ascends moderately to the north before reaching an open area at 0.3 mi. (0.5 km). Red DEC trail markers now guide you over an easier path, which becomes moderate again before arriving at the first lookout, to the left, at 0.5 mi. (0.8 km).

Still ascending, a second lookout is found at 0.7 mi. (1.1 km), at which the trail makes a sharp right turn just before two angular boulders on a ledge.

Most people continue up the now-steep trail to a third viewpoint at 0.9 mi. (1.4 km), but few continue on the vague trail beyond that climbs another 0.3 mi. (0.5 km) before petering out. However, for those who enjoy a good scramble, the mountain ridge offers another 2.0 mi. (3.2 km) of bushwhack and ledges.

Whiteface Mt., Silver Lake, Taylor Pond, and Catamount Mt. are but a few of the excellent sightings possible from this short climb. Take lunch and pick some blueberries for dessert in season.

49. Azure Mountain (Blue Mountain)
Round-trip Time: 1 hr. 30 min.
Round-trip Distance: 2.0 mi. (3.2 km)
Elevation Change: Estimated 944 ft. (288 m)
Summit Elevation: 2518 ft. (770 m)
Difficulty: Short, but very steep.
Map: Lake Ozonia 7.5'; or Santa Clara 15'

Another of the outpost mountains, Azure (French for *blue*) provides a magnificent view of the distant high peaks from the north. This is in sharp contrast to the numerous small bodies of water found at its base. Altogether one is rewarded with a striking picture from climbing this small peak.

Access to the trailhead is off Rt. 458, 4 mi. (6.5 km) south of St. Regis Falls or about 3 mi. (4.9 km) north of Santa Clara. At this point, Blue Mountain Road is reached on the south side of the road. Blue Mountain Road is a broad gravel road in excellent condition.

Follow Blue Mountain Road for 6.7 mi. (10.9 km) to a spring on the right, opposite a home. A small entrance road is reached at 0.4 mi. (0.6 km), also on the right side of the road. A parking area is located a short distance along the entrance road and the trailhead is at the far end of it. A picnic table with fireplace is found beyond a gate and 0.3 mi. (0.5 km) down a woods road. This is all that remains of a former fire observer's cabin.

Entering a mature maple forest, the first few hundred feet of path rise gradually. Almost all of the rest of the trail, however, varies from moderately steep to steep. It is a short but rigorous climb. The trail is marked with both red DEC markers and yellow paint blazes. To ease the ascent, numerous switchbacks have been built into the trail. For your walking safety and to prevent erosion of the mountain, follow the official trail. Extensive trail work has made this a very nice foot trail on which to negotiate the mountain. Stone steps, switchbacks, gravel, and waterbars all add to the quality of the trail.

The trail moderates for the last few hundred feet. The tower is soon seen ahead. Walking through high brush and long grass, you are at the tower before you can see far into the distance.

Beyond the tower open rock provides an exquisite panorama. Below you are numerous ponds. The deep blue bodies of water seem to be surrounded by a hundred shades of green.

Out to the south are Whiteface, Giant, the Great Range, Marcy, the McIntyres, and the Sewards. Closer in are dozens of lesser ridges. Huge Debar Mountain stands out in the east. The thin ribbon of water to the north is the St. Lawrence River.

The huge boulder on the edge of the drop-off on the west side of the open rock is another of nature's mysteries. Why did the glaciers of the last ice age choose that spot to leave such a giant rock? Perhaps it is to remind us of the great power of their forces.

50. Debar Mountain
Round-trip Time: 4 hrs. 30 min.
Round-trip Distance: 7.3 mi. (11.9 km)
Elevation Change: 1726 ft. (528 m)
Summit Elevation: 3300 ft. (1009 m)
Difficulty: Generally easy, but the last half mile is as steep as anything in the Adirondacks that has a trail.
Map: Debar Mountain 7.5'; or Santa Clara 15'

Far to the north, Debar Mountain sits beside beautiful Meacham Lake. Surrounded by state forests, she is isolated. Rising 800 ft. (245 m) in the last 0.5 mi. (0.8 km), the peak offers a mixture of easy woods walking and rugged climbing. Plan to make use of the wonderful beach at Meacham Lake.

Access to the mountain trail is from Rt. 30 at Meacham Lake Public Campground, 18 mi. (29.2 km) south of Malone. Follow either entrance road off Rt. 30 to the campground toll booth. A small day-use charge is required to enter the campground.

Proceed straight ahead from the toll booth 0.2 mi. (0.3 km) until you see a small sign on the left indicating the turn for Debar Mountain. This is the left-hand turn for Campsites 21–52. Just past Campsite 37, bear right onto the sandy road which branches off. At 0.4 mi. (0.6 km) along this road, you'll arrive at a large parking area and the gate which marks the beginning of the trail. Posted distances seem exaggerated.

Red trail markers take you along a woods road through a mixed forest occasionally heavy with balsam fir. The way is almost flat in this section. At 0.9 mi. (1.4 km), turn left at the junction. A small Debar Mountain trail sign high in a tree points the way.

From here the grade varies from gradual to moderately steep. In general, it steepens gradually as you progress. At 2.3 mi. (3.8 km) it would appear the trail will take you right into a boulder, but it swings to the left and continues on to a height of land at 2.5 mi. (4.0 km).

The level stretch soon ends and the trail descends slightly to a small creek. It then resumes its gradual upgrade course. A lean-to, on the left, is passed at 2.9 mi. (47 km). Your objective can be seen to the right front from this location. Soon after, the remains of the burnt-out fire observer's cabin are reached. Its small clearing is growing in from disuse.

The long walk to this point has been relatively easy; from here on, care must be taken. The trail narrows and becomes a rocky path. Before long the way becomes very steep, and it is frequently necessary to use your hands to get over some of the rocks. Eventually the trail moderates, and for the last five minutes you can catch your breath as you stride through a sweet-smelling stand of balsam fir.

Circling the base of the bald rock, which once held a fire tower, you finally reach the open and rocky summit.

Meacham Lake dominates the scene. Clear Pond is to its right. Far to the right is Deer River Flow. The High Peaks are to your extreme left, in the southeast. Whiteface, St. Regis, Morris, and Ampersand mountains can be spotted. Azure, Loon Lake Mountain, and Lyon Mountain are to the north.

Portions of the trail and much of the campground seem ideal for cross-country skiing. The upper stretches of the trail would require some mountain-skiing skill and perhaps would be best done on snowshoes. Only those with considerable experience should try to snowshoe beyond the lean-to.

Index

Listings are entered by proper name first. Words like mount, mountain, lake, etc. follow the proper name.

Abanakee, Lake 46
Adirondack Mt. Club 27
Adirondack Mt. Club
   Headquarters 28
Adirondack Range 23
Adirondak Loj 27–28, 94
Aiden Lair 64
Ampersand Mt. 85–86
Andia-to-roc-tee 32
Arab, Mt. 107
Archer & Anna Huntington
   Wildlife Station 70
Ausable River, East Branch 77
Avalanche Pass 60
Azure Mt. 113–114

Baker Mt. 86–87
Balanced Rocks 79–80
Bald Mt. 53–54
Barnum Brook 96–97
Bear Brook 77
Bear Mt. 104–105
Beaver Brook 43–44
Beaver Meadow 57
Big Bay 46
Big Crow Mt. 83
Big Slide Mt. 76
Black Bear Mt.
   Eagle Bay 57–59
   Cranberry Lake 104–105
Black Ledges 30
Black Mt 29, 30, 36–37
Black Mt. Pond 37
Blue Mt. 60–61
Boreas River 64, 66
Boquet Range 23
Boquet River 73
Brandy Brook 104
Brandy Brook Flow 102–104
Brothers, The 74–77
Brown Mt. 29, 30, 32
Brownell's Camp 47, 49
Bubb Lake 56
Buck Mt. 29, 34–36
Buell, Mt. 44
Bullhead Mt. 47

Burntbridge Pond 104
Butterfly House 96
Butternut Brook 34

Camp Peggy O'Brien 28
Campfires 21
Canadian Shield 23
Cascade Lake 56
Cascade Pond 62–63
Cat Mt. 100–102
Cat Mt. Pond 102
Catskill Mts. 33, 38
Cedar River 50
Circuit Trail 55–56
Chain Ponds 57
Champlain, Lake 23, 37, 109
Chimney Mt. 46–48
Chubb River 92–93
Clay Meadows 29–33
Cod Pond 49–50, 51
Colden, Lake 65
Copperas Pond 90–92
Cowhorn Junction 102
Cranberry Lake 99, 102
Cranberry Lake
   Public Campground 104
Cranberry Lake Wild Forest 102
Crane Mt. 29, 39–41
Crane Mt. Pond 39
Crane Pond 41
Crossett Pond 34
Crows, The 83–84
Crystal Brook 77

Dayton Creek 49
Dead Creek 100
Dead Creek Flow 100
Debar Mt. 114–115
Deer Brook 77
Deer Leap 30
Desolate Brook 42
Dog Pond Loop 104

Eagle Bay 53
East Dix Mt. 74
East Inlet 104

East Stony Creek 47, 49
Echo Cliffs 44–46
Eighth Lake 53
equipment 21

Fifth Peak 29
fire towers 22
First Brother 76
First Peak 29, 32–33
Five Mile Mt. 29, 30–32
Five Mile Point 32
Five Ponds Wilderness Area 100
Follensby Pond 85
Forest Ecology Trail 96
Foster's Observatory 53

Ganienkeh 54
Garden, The 74, 76–77
George, Lake 23, 29–37
Giant Mt. 78
Gilligan Mt. 73–74
Glasby Pond 102
Goodnow Mt. 64, 70–71
Grace Camp 28
Great Sacandaga Lake, The ... 38, 47, 49
Green Mt. 78

Hadley Mt. 38
Hamilton Mt. 46
Harris Lake 63
Harrisburg Lake 65
Haystack Mt. (Ray Brook) 89–91
Heart Lake 24, 27, 94
Helderbergs 38
Heron Brook 96
Heron Marsh 96
Hewitt Eddy 66
Higgins Bay 46
High Peaks 74
High Peaks Info Center 27
Hill of Storms 60
Hill of Wind 78
Hopkins Mt. 77–78
Hough Mt. 74
Huckleberry Mt. 29, 30
Hudson River, The 38, 62
Hurricane Mt. 72, 78–79
hypothermia 18

Indian Lake 23, 43
Indian Pass Trail 94
Inman Pond 34

Janacks Landing 100
Jo, Mt. 93–95

Johns Brook 76–77
Johns Brook Lodge 28, 77
Juliet Brook 76

Kattskill Bay 34
Kayaderosseras Range 23
Keene Valley 73
Kings Flow 46–47

Lac du St. Sacrament 33
Lake of the Blessed Sacrament 33
Lake Region 23, 53
Land of Flint 54
Lapland Pond 37
Lewey Lake 43
Little Buck Mt. 34
Little Crow Mt. 83
Little Ray Brook 89
Long Lake 23, 60
Lower Hogtown 34
Luzerne Range 23
Lyon Mt. 110–111

maps 13
Marcy, Mt. 65
McComb Mt. 74
McKenzie Mt. 89
Meacham Lake 114
Meacham Lake
    Public Campground 114
metric measurement units 13
Middle Saranac Lake 85
Minerva 65
Minnow Pond 60
Mohegan Lake 57
Montcalm Point 29, 33
Mont. St. Louis 53
Moody Pond 87
Moss Lake 54–57
Moss Lake Camp for Girls 54
Mossy Cascade Brook 77–78
Mossy Cascade Brook Falls 78
Mother Bunch Islands 30
Mountain Belt 23
Mountain House 79, 83
Mud Pond 60

Narrows, The 33, 35, 37
Nature Conservancy 54
Newcomb 65
Newcomb Visitor
    Interpretive Center 65, 70
No-do-ne-yo 78
Noonmark Mt. 82–83
Northville–Placid Trail 47, 49, 51,
                                    63, 92–93

Northwest Bay 29–33

Ouluska Pass 86
Owen Pond 90–92
Owen Pond Brook 91
Oxbow Lake 46

Panther Mt. 44
Paradox Lake 29
Paul Smiths 85
Paul Smiths Visitor
    Interpretive Center 96
Pharaoh Mt. 29, 41–42
Phelps Trail 77
Pilot Knob 34
Peninsula Brook 70
Piseco Lake 44
Pitchoff Mt. 79–80
Placid, Lake 27, 85
Plains Trail 102
Pohquis-Moosie 109
Poke-O-Moonshine 109–110
Pond Mt. 53
Putnam Farm 39

Queer Lake 57

Rankin Pond 64–65
Ranney Trail 78
Raquette Lake 53
rattlesnakes 29
Ray Brook 88
Rich Lake 70
Rich Lumber Company 100
Rock Pond 62
Rondaxe Mt. 53–54
Roosevelt Memorial Tablet 69
Round Mt. 82
Round Pond
    Kings Flow 47
    Dix Trail 82
    Lake George 37

safety 19, 22
Santanoni Preserve 71
Saranac Lake 85
Sawyer Mt. 50–51
Scarface Mt. 87–89
Schroon Lake 42
Schroon Range 23
Second Brother 76
Shingle Mill Falls 96
Silverculture Trail 96
Silver Lake Mt. 111–113
site types 24–25

Sis Lake 56
Slide Brook 76
Snowy Mt. 43–44
South Pond 60
Spectacle Pond 42
Split Rock Falls 73
Spread Eagle Mt. 78
Spruce Mt. 38
Spy Lake 46
Squaw Brook 44
Stagecoach Rock 80–82
St. Lawrence River 62, 99
St. Regis Mt. 96–98
Sucker Brook 70
Summit Stewards 27
Sunday Rock 99
Sunday Rock Association 99
Sunrise Mt. 73
Sunrise Trail 73

Tahawus Club 69
Tenant Creek 47
Three Sisters Mts. 46
Third Brother 74, 76
Tirrell Mt. 60
Tirrell Pond 60
Tongue Mt. 60
Tongue Mt. Range 29–34
Top Ridge 98
To-war-loon-da 60
trail manners 21

Vanderwhacker Brook 67
Vanderwhacker Mt. 64, 66–69
Visitor Interpretive Center ... 65, 70, 96

Wanakena 99
Wanika Falls 92–93
West Mountain Ridge 38
Wilcox Lake 47–49
Wilcox Mt. 49
Willis Lake 49
Winch Pond 91
Windfall Pond 55–57
winter hiking 11–12
Witch's Bay 99

INDEX OF PEOPLE

Adler, Felix 82
Agassiz, Louis 85

Beauchamp, William 109
Brown, Louis 82

Carnes, Wilfred 82
Colvin, Verplanck 42, 60, 110
Cook, Fred 81
Cook, Rev. Thomas 110
Cooper, James Fenimore 33
Cuomo, Mario 54

Dewey, Melvil 94
Dunning, Alvah 53

Emerson, Ralph Waldo 85

Foster, Nat 53

Huntington, Archer and Anna 70

Jogues, Fr. Isaac 32
Johnson, Gen. William 33

King George II 33

Marshall, Robert 11
McKinley, John 69
Merril, Charles 110
Mohawk Nation 54
Montcalm, Marquis de 33
Morgan, James Pierpont 57

Native American 54

O'Brien, "Fitch" 81

Phelps, Orson Schofield 73
Post, Marjorie Merriweather 98

Remington, Frederic 99
Rice, Walter Channing 86
Roblee, Ike 81
Rogers, Donald 82
Rondeau, Noah John 86
Roosevelt, Theodore 69

Schenectady Chapter, ADK 74
Scofield, Josephine 94
Seymour, "French Louie" 43
Stillman, William James 85
Stoddard, Seneca Ray 36
Stoner, Nick 43
Street, Alfred Billings 60

Van Hoevenberg, Henry 27, 93

Wickham, Robert 71
Wood, Reuben 99

About the Author

Bruce Wadsworth is a retired science educator in Lake Placid, New York. He holds degrees from Alfred University, Syracuse University and the State University at Albany. He has participated in National Science Foundation Institutes in geology of North America at Vassar and in cytology and biochemistry at Alfred University. In addition, he took part in in-depth studies of Adirondack biosystems at the Cranberry Lake Biological Station, SUNY College of Environmental Science and Forestry.

His family of four became "46ers" after climbing each of the High Peaks together, and Wadsworth has been an end-to-ender on the Northville–Placid Trail four times. Early spring usually finds him clearing hiking trails. Special interests include wilderness preservation and Adirondack history. He is an active member of the Adirondack Mountain Club (ADK) and the author of several ADK publications.

Working for wilderness and loving it.

JOIN US!

We are a nonprofit membership organization that brings together people with interests in recreation, conservation, and environmental education in the New York State Forest Preserve. Our 35,000 members pursue a wide range of outdoor activities, including hiking, canoeing, backpacking, climbing, skiing, and snowshoeing. Many also join ADK to support our work on trails and in the halls of government, and thus lend their voices to protecting New York's Adirondack and Catskill Parks.

Other benefits include:
- receipt of *Adirondac* six times per year
- discounts on ADK publications, educational workshops, and wilderness lodges
- the opportunity to join a local chapter and enjoy its outings and activities
- the opportunity to apply for the ADK Visa card

BACKCOUNTRY EDUCATION & STEWARDSHIP

ADK is a leader in teaching outdoor skills and promoting recreational activities consistent with the region's wild character. Thus the Club offers workshops ranging from field natural history to hiking, canoeing, and skiing, and orienteering and wilderness first aid.

In addition, ADKers are known for "giving back" to the places that have nurtured them, by participating in extensive work on trails throughout the New York State Forest Preserve.

For more information about the Adirondacks or about ADK:
Information Center & Headquarters
814 Goggins Road, Lake George, NY 12845-4117
(518) 668-4447
Exit 21 off I-87 ("the Northway"), 9N south

Mon.–Sat., 8:30 A.M.–5 P.M.

For lodge, cabin, or campground reservations on ADK's Heart Lake property in the High Peaks region, write or call:
Adirondack Mountain Club
Box 867
Lake Placid, NY 12946-0867
(518) 523-3441
(9 A.M.–7 P.M. daily)